U IS FOR UNICORN

Eileen Campbell

Sally Milner Publishing

EDITORIAL
MANAGING EDITOR
Judy Poulos
EDITORIAL ASSISTANT
Ella Martin
EDITORIAL COORDINATOR
Margaret Kelly
EDITORIAL & PRODUCTION ASSISTANT
Heather Straton

PHOTOGRAPHY
Richard Weinstein
STYLING
Kathy Tripp

PRODUCTION AND DESIGN
PRODUCTION DIRECTOR
Anna Maguire
PRODUCTION COORDINATOR
Meredith Johnston
DESIGN MANAGER
Drew Buckmaster
PRODUCTION EDITOR
Sheridan Packer
COVER DESIGN
Lulu Dougherty
CONCEPT DESIGN
Jenny Pace

PUBLISHED BY Sally Milner Publishing Pty Ltd
P.O. Box 2104
Bowral NSW 2576
AUSTRALIA
www.sallymilner.com.au

PRINTED BY Toppan Printing Co. China
REPRINTED 1999, 2000
© Eileen Campbell

U IS FOR UNICORN
ISBN 1 86351 271 3

This book belongs to
Ms Joan Messenger

Contents

For my grandchildren: Lachlan and Laura, Maddison and Bryce.

ACKNOWLEDGMENTS

To Judy Poulos and Karen Fail from J B Fairfax Press – a big thankyou for all the support and encouragement so cheerfully given.
Thank you also to:
Richard Weinstein for truly excellent photography; Madeira Threads for supplying some of the threads for this work; Sue Broadbent for typing the manuscript and managing to decipher my scribblings;
Sue Trytell for suggestions and advice on the Bolster and Welcome projects; my sons, Derek, Alan and Neil and my daughters-in-law, Alison, Katie-Anne and Sarah, for their loving encouragement and support always.
And to Ernie, for everything – without him this book would not have happened.
Eileen

The Appliqué Method

CUTTING THE BLOCKS

The block measurements are given without seam allowances.

Cut the blocks to be appliquéd a little larger than is actually required, to allow for shrinkage. For example, a 26 cm x 26 cm (10 in x 10 in) block would normally be cut 27 cm x 27 cm (10¹/2 in x 10¹/2 in) to allow for seams. To allow the extra for shrinkage, cut the block 28 cm x 28 cm (11 in x 11 in). Mark the correct block size on it with a dressmaker's pencil or something similar, then complete the appliqué. Trim the block to the correct size PLUS seam allowances, before assembling the quilt.

TRACING THE DESIGN

Note: All the block designs for the Medieval Inspirations Quilt are given at half size. Enlarge them on a photocopier at 200 per cent, before tracing them.

All the appliqué projects in this book have used Vliesofix. Vliesofix is a double-sided fusible webbing with tracing paper on one side. It makes appliquéing very simple, provided you remember one thing: your design must be traced on the Vliesofix IN REVERSE.

To reverse the image, hold or tape the design onto a light box or a window with the light shining through it. You will then be able to trace your designs on the reverse side of the paper very easily.

You will need to trace some designs facing both ways, such as some leaves and flowers or the gryphon used for the quilting pattern on Bryce's quilt on page 64.

Each part of a motif that will be on a different fabric must be drawn separately. Where one piece adjoins another, allow a margin of up to 5 mm (¹/4 in) on the piece that will underlap the front piece. This is necessary so that all the pieces can be firmly stitched to the backing fabric without any gaps or raw edges showing. It is easiest to draw in a dotted line for the underlap on the original design and include it on your

Step 1: Trace the pattern and mark the underlaps.

Step 2: Trace all the pieces separately, in reverse, onto Vliesofix.

tracing. Trace the pieces (including the extensions of the reversed image) onto the smooth side of the Vliesofix. If you have many pieces to be cut from the one fabric – for example, a group of flowers – you can trace them in a block and handle them as one image at this stage. Cut out the traced pieces leaving a small margin all around.

CUTTING OUT THE PIECES

Using a dry iron on a medium setting, press the rough side of the Vliesofix onto the back of the appliqué fabric. Remember, if you are using synthetic or delicate fabrics, protect them from direct heat. Cut out the traced shapes exactly from the fabric.

When you have cut out the appliqué pieces, arrange them on the backing fabric. At this stage, you may find you need more or less pieces, such as flowers or leaves. Be prepared to adjust your design according to the overall effect.

Peel the tracing paper backing from the Vliesofix on each of the appliqué pieces. Making sure that all the underlaps are in place and each piece is situated correctly, use a dry iron at a medium setting and fuse the pieces onto the background.

STABILISERS

Back your work with an iron-on stabiliser extending 2.5 cm (1 in) beyond all the appliqué pieces. This gives a firm base on which to appliqué and do free machine-embroidery. The stabiliser is torn away after the stitching is completed.

If you have a large design, it is easier to manoeuvre the appliqué under the machine if you work in sections and stabilise areas as you go. Stitch the pieces in place and complete any machine-embroidery.

Take care when you tear the stabiliser away from any embroidery. Hold the embroidery stitching with one finger while you tear carefully around it.

Iron-on Tearaway is one product which gives a very firm base; however, you must be careful not to 'burn' any stabiliser on or it is very difficult to remove. Use just sufficient

heat to adhere it to the fabric, then tear it away immediately after stitching. Another iron-on stabiliser looks more like paper with one shiny side. It is the shiny side that is ironed against the fabric. This does not give as much support for heavy stitching, but tears away much more easily. There are other products available, so experiment to see which type you prefer working with. All of them are temporary supports and are torn away after stitching is completed.

Another stabiliser is iron-on Vilene, but this is not torn away. It is used for the three-dimensional appliqués or in any place where you want the extra support to remain permanently. Medium-weight to heavyweight iron-on Vilene is best. However, the lightweight one gives a lovely soft finish and you can use two or three layers to give more stiffness.

THREE-DIMENSIONAL APPLIQUE

This technique adds great interest to the quilt and is used for flowers, leaves or creatures which will be held in place at one or more points, leaving some parts of the appliqué free-standing.

Follow the steps for the appliqué method up to the cutting out of the pieces, then proceed as follows: cut a piece of backing fabric large enough to hold all the appliqués plus 1 cm (3/8 in) all round. Choose an appropriate fabric for the backing if it is likely to show.

Depending on how firm you want the appliqués to be, cut either one (or two) pieces

Step 3: Cut out the pieces, leaving a small margin all round, and fuse to the back of the appliqué fabric.

Step 4. Cut out the shapes exactly from the fabric.

Step 5: Arrange the appliqués on the background with the underlaps in place. Back with stabiliser, then satin stitch.

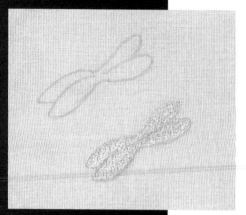

Draw the design in pencil on the heat-vanishing muslin (above) then stitch (below).

The motifs are fused to the backing with one or two layers of Vilene and stitched.

Cut-out appliqué pieces are assembled and stitched in place.

of iron-on Vilene the same size as the backing fabric and fuse it (or them) to the backing fabric. Peel the tracing paper from the Vliesofix on the appliqués and arrange them on top of the Vilene. Fuse them into place and satin stitch around the edges. Some machine- or hand-embroidery can be done at this stage. Keep in mind you will probably use further embroidery to attach the appliqué to the background.

Cut out the appliqués. It is easiest to use a small pair of sharp scissors and angle them underneath the work, taking care not to cut the appliqué threads. Leaving the tiniest possible margin of backing will help, and these tiny pieces fall or pull away afterwards. If you do cut a thread – as nearly always happens – use a fray stopper or a drop of clear craft glue to prevent the stitches from unravelling.

If the cut edges of the Vilene are too visible, colour them carefully with a fabric marker pen. If the project will not be washed, then ordinary felt-tipped markers will do.

FREE-FORM PADDED APPLIQUES

This technique can be used when you want even more definition or a three-dimensional effect. Prepare the pieces as for the three-dimensional appliqué, but using only one layer of iron-on Vilene. Cut a piece of iron-on Pellon the same size as the backing fabric. If iron-on Pellon is not available, cut a piece of Vliesofix the same size as ordinary Pellon and fuse them together. Peel off the paper and you now have iron-on Pellon, which you can fuse onto the iron-on Vilene. Use Glad Bake between the Pellon and the iron. Glad Bake is a baking and cooking paper with a non-stick coating.

Peel the tracing paper from the appliqué pieces, arrange them on the Pellon and fuse them in place, again using Glad Bake. Satin stitch round the edges and complete any embroidery needed at this stage, then cut out and finish the pieces in the same way as the unpadded appliqué.

ATTACHING THE PIECES

Flowers and leaves can be attached to the background using the embroidery for their stamens or leaf veins and the appropriately coloured machine-embroidery rayon thread. Butterflies, bats or birds are attached by free machine-stitching around their bodies. Depending on size, the wings can be left free, or caught down at the tips, perhaps angling the wing against the background.

Monofilament nylon thread is very good for attaching creatures, as it is not obvious.

Bodies of creatures such as the dragon or brolga can be further padded as they are attached. Stitch around half of the body, then insert a very small amount of dacron filling. Push it into place using a satay stick or something similar, then finish stitching. Attach three-dimensional and most padded pieces after the quilting is completed. However, flowers and leaves attached before quilting, then quilted under the petals, tend to stand up and contrast very well with flowers appliquéd directly onto the background.

MEASUREMENTS

All the measurements in this book are given in both metric and imperial terms. These are NOT interchangeable.

It does not matter whether you choose to work in metric or imperial measurements, but whichever you choose, you must stick with all the way through and not change from one to the other, or your quilt will not come together properly.

For the Medieval Inspirations quilt, the block designs are given at half size. Enlarge them on a photocopier at 200 per cent before tracing them.

Depending on which measurement system you use, some of the designs may need very minor manipulation to fit on the block, such as altering the angle of a line or having one less leaf. Once you have traced and cut out the appliqué pieces for a block, lay the pieces out on the background before you begin to stitch.

Stitching

SATIN STITCH

What you are trying to achieve here are zigzag stitches that are close enough together to appear to be a solid line, but not so close that the stitches bunch up and jam the machine. Because there can be a mixture of fabrics for each project, use a piece of stabiliser-backed fabric from your project with a couple of appliqué scraps fused to it as a test piece. This will allow you to test tension, stitches and thread colour.

For the projects in this book, the stitch width was between 1.5 mm and 2 mm (up to 1/16 in). If you have large appliqués, a wider satin stitch can be used. At less than 1 mm (1/32 in), the satin stitch becomes too narrow to hold the appliqué in place. For something very small, it is best to use free machine-stitching. The satin stitch length should be set very fine, but still with enough length so that, if you let go of the fabric, the feed dogs will push the fabric through the machine without any problem. Your stitches should rest mostly on the appliqué, only just coming over onto the background fabric.

Plan the stitching order. Begin with the shapes that are furthest back and work to the front. Most starting and stopping points will be covered by subsequent stitching.

Hold and control your work mainly with your left hand. Place the first two fingers in a V shape on either side of the presser foot, exerting a little pressure away from the presser foot to keep your work flat. Your right hand is then free to change the stitch width as you sew.

Begin and end the stitching with a few fastening stitches on one spot, or pull the top thread through to the back and tie it off.

To change the angle stitching round a curve, stop with the needle down in the wide side of the curve, lift the presser foot, turn the work slightly and take a few more stitches. Repeat this pivoting step as many times as you find it necessary to complete the curve smoothly. With experience, you will find you can control your stitching at a fair speed, eliminating some of the stopping and starting by turning your work as you go.

Left: Satin stitch is used to stitch down the appliqués.

ADJUSTING THE TENSION

The top tension will need to be adjusted to produce a smooth, even satin stitch without any bobbin stitch showing.

To do this, loosen the top tension a little. For example, if the normal setting is 4, then reduce it to 3. If your machine has + or – on the tension dial, then move it towards the minus sign. You may find you need to reduce tension even more than this. Stitch a test piece, using stabilised fabric with contrasting coloured threads in the top and bobbin, then take it out of the machine and look at the back. You should have the top thread colour showing down both sides of the bobbin thread. Probably, there will be more top colour showing along one side than the other. If the top thread is not being pulled through enough, then reduce the tension further and try again. Keep this test piece and write your settings on it so that you have it as a reference.

On some machines, threading the bobbin thread through the special hole for buttonholes has the same effect as loosening the tension. You may or may not have to adjust the top tension a little more. Also check your machine manual as to the recommendations for satin stitching.

MAKING POINTS

Using a 1.5–2 mm (up to 1/16 in) stitch, it is not necessary to taper points on leaves etc. Continue to the top of the point, leave the needle down and turn your work. Raise the needle and reposition the work so that your first stitching in the other direction covers the previous couple of stitches. This will give you a blunt point which is very easy to do without affecting the good appearance of the motif. Sometimes, it does not matter if your stitching goes a little off the line and moves too far onto the appliqué – for example, if it is a leaf or flower and the basic shape is not altered appreciably. If this is the

Above: Free machine-embroidery is used to embellish the appliqué.

case, lift the excess appliqué fabric with your fingernail, then use a pair of very sharp scissors to trim off the piece.

If trimming the appliqué will spoil the shape or you have stitched too far off the appliqué and it is no longer held down, then you must take the stitching out and re-stitch it. The simplest method is to turn your work to the back and, with a small pair of sharp scissors, cut through the bobbin thread of the satin stitching. Turn your work to the right side and pull the top thread above where you have cut – it will unravel like magic.

FREE MACHINE-EMBROIDERY

Free machine-embroidery can be used for embellishing the appliqués, stitching highlights and as an alternative method for holding down some of the appliqués. It is especially useful for very small pieces.

You will need a darning foot for your sewing machine. You will also need to be able to lower the feed dogs or to cover them with a plate. If you cannot lower or cover the feed dogs, sticking masking tape over them can be a solution.

Using the darning foot

Although it is possible to take the normal sewing foot off the machine and embroider without a foot at all, it is much easier and safer to use a darning foot. A darning foot usually has a spring that allows it to move up and down while you sew. It gives support as the needle makes the stitch but allows you to move the fabric freely at the same time.

On most Husqvarna machines, you must turn to the darning symbol which will release the pressure of the machine foot on the fabric. Some Pfaff machines have a cradle position on the presser lever that lets you free machine-stitch, without lowering the foot right onto the fabric. Check with your machine instruction manual or sewing machine dealer, as different makes and models have different adjustments.

Whichever machine and darning foot you have, it is essential to lower the presser foot lever before you begin sewing, otherwise you will end up with a terrible tangle of threads on the underside of your work.

Using a hoop

Using a stabiliser on the back of your work generally gives sufficient support when small amounts of free machine-stitching are to be used. For more extensive embroidery, the work should be in a hoop. A spring hoop works well, especially when the fabric is already stabilised.

Working with a hoop for machine-embroidery is done in the opposite way to hand-embroidery. The fabric is placed at the bottom of the hoop so that it will lie flat on the bed of the machine.

A plastic and metal spring hoop – either 13 cm (5 in) or 18 cm (7 in) – is very easy to work with. It can be moved quickly and easily from one area to another and, with the fabric already stabilised, you do not have to be concerned about a very tight tension in the hoop. If you are doing more elaborate embroidery, especially without a stabiliser, you will need to use a wooden hoop with a binding on the inside ring, which can be tightened by a screw at the side.

To use a spring hoop, lay the plastic ring on a flat surface, then place your fabric over the top. Squeeze the two handles on the metal spring together and fit the spring into the plastic ring, so that the fabric is stretched evenly all round. There will be one place just in front of the spring handles where you are unable to get the correct tension in the fabric. Just be aware of this and position the area you are to embroider away from it.

If you are new to machine-embroidery, it is worth practising on some sample swatches.

Free machine-stitching

To begin, set the machine for straight stitching with the stitch width and length at 0. Tension should be normal to begin with, but you may have to decrease it a little, depending on your stitching. Try it on your test piece. Lower the presser foot and bring the bobbin thread to the top by taking one stitch and pulling on the top thread to bring the bobbin thread up. Hold both threads to the back of your work and make two or three stitches which will hold both threads. You can now cut off the threads. Begin to stitch, moving the work in any direction. Coordinating the movement of the work with your hands, and the speed with the foot control, you will be able to control the size, length and direction of your stitching. It is best if you can maintain a fairly fast speed, but this will come with practise. It is not necessary to turn your work, as you can stitch in any direction. This is the same technique which is used in free machine-quilting, where it is simply not possible to turn the whole quilt under the machine. It is best to practise keeping the work straight from the start.

When using a hoop, hold the edges of the hoop while stitching. Without a hoop, place one hand on either side of the presser foot to hold and guide the work flat on the bed of the machine.

Above: Heat-vanishing muslin was used to create the lyre bird's tail feathers.

USING HEAT-VANISHING MUSLIN (THERMOGAZE)

This technique was used for the lyre-bird tails on the 'Welcome' project on page 55. Thermogaze (a brand name) or heat-vanishing muslin can be put into a hoop and embroidered. Subsequent ironing turns the muslin into a brown powder which can be brushed away.

When embroidering on Thermogaze, use the same thread through the needle and in the bobbin. Make sure that all your embroidery lines are connected so that your piece will not fall apart when the supporting backing is removed. You can draw on Thermogaze easily with a pencil, if you need guidelines.

Put the embroidered Thermogaze between two pieces of Glad Bake when you press it. This protects the threads from direct heat and catches all the powdery bits as they crumble away. A nail brush is handy for removing the last of the powdered Thermogaze. Store Thermogaze in a dark place to prevent it deteriorating.

To attach this embroidery, before or after quilting, use either the same coloured thread or clear monofilament thread, and free machine-stitch it in place, leaving some areas unattached for a three-dimensional effect.

Above: The whiskers on the rabbits could be hand- or machine-embroidered.

HAND-EMBROIDERY

If you would rather hand-embroider the appliqués or use some hand-embroidery in conjunction with the machine-embroidery, then the three stitches that you will find most useful are stem stitch, chain stitch and French knots.

Stem stitch can decorate flowers, create stems or add highlights of all sorts.

Chain stitch is excellent for birds' legs. Outline the legs with a very narrow (1.5 mm (1/16 in)) machine satin stitch, then fill in the shapes with fine rows of chain stitch, using metallic thread.

French knots can be used in flower centres and on wings. The possibilities are endless and, of course, many other stitches can also be used.

MACHINE-QUILTING

Prepare your backing, which should be 5 cm (2 in) bigger all round than the quilt top. Lay it out, wrong side up, on a smooth, flat surface, such as a large table or the floor. Pull the edges of the backing taut, but do not stretch them, and tape down the corners and centres with masking tape. Use a couple more pieces of tape on each side for a large piece. Place the batting on top and smooth it out. If you have to join batting, butt the edges together and sew them with a diagonal basting stitch. Do not overlap them or you will have a ridge in the finished quilt. A hair dryer helps remove fold marks and fluff up the batting. Tape it into position, then place your thoroughly pressed quilt top, right side up, on top of the batting,

making sure the centre of the quilt top edges line up with the centre points on the edges of the batting. Tape it in place.

Beginning at the centre of one edge and working to one corner, then working from the centre edge again to the other corner, put in 2.5 cm (1 in) safety pins, about 5 cm (2 in) apart. Move to the opposite side of the quilt and repeat, then do the last two sides. You will now have safety pins right round the edge of the quilt.

Working from the edges towards the centre of the quilt, place safety pins 8-10 cm (3-4 in) apart over the entire quilt. For a large quilt you will need four to five hundred pins. Try not to place pins where you intend to stitch, for example in the ditch on sashings. Avoid pinning appliqués if at all possible – pin around them. Be very careful when pinning silk, as it marks so easily. Pin against the appliqués or in a spot where it will be covered by quilting. Use the back of a teaspoon or a small paté knife to lift the pin as you close it. It is much faster and saves your fingers. Remove the tape and you are ready for quilting. Pinning in this manner and taking the pins out as you stitch is much easier than pulling basting threads out from under machine-quilting.

What threads to use

For a quilting line that gives texture without making a feature of the thread, use monofilament thread – clear on light colours and smoke-coloured on dark ones. Monofilament thread is difficult to tie into a knot as it is quite springy. Begin and end your quilting lines with five or six stitches placed very close together – almost on 0.

In the bobbin, use a polycotton or polyester thread that tones with the backing fabric. Depending on what your project will be used for, you have many other choices of quilting thread. There are also many colours of machine-quilting threads available. You might like to use machine-embroidery rayon or even metallic thread, or possibly a combination of two or more of these. Use a size 80 needle, a Metalfil needle or a quilting needle – whichever suits your thread.

Which sewing foot to use

For straight-line quilting, either in the ditch, as decoration or on gentle curves, a walking foot is excellent and should be used if possible. A walking foot feeds the layers of fabric evenly though the machine, eliminating bubbles on either side of the quilt sandwich. Some Pfaff machines have an even-feed foot built into the machine instead of a walking foot, and if your machine has this it should be engaged.

For outline-quilting or free-motion quilting (Cornelli work or stippling) a darning foot is necessary. The method is the same as that described for free machine-embroidery.

Marking the quilt top

The choice of marker depends on the colour of the fabric and the type of design to be marked. Always test the marker on a scrap of fabric first to check for visibility and how easily the marks can be removed.

Some suggestions are a silver pencil, a fine H lead pencil, a coloured pencil a couple of shades darker than the fabric, tailor's chalk, quilters' tape 6 mm ($1/4$ in) wide, a chalk wheel or a water-soluble blue pen. If you use a water-soluble pen, make sure it is really soluble and wash the marks out of the quilt thoroughly, as soon as possible.

For marking patterns such as the gryphons on Bryce's quilt on page 64 or the border on the Z Flower Quilt on page 73, the easiest way is to first trace them onto greaseproof paper, using an H or HB lead pencil. Do not use a very soft lead pencil, as the lead tends to mark the quilt when it is stitched. Leave a margin of at least 4 cm (1$1/2$ in) all round, then use 2.5 cm (1 in) safety pins to pin it to the area to be quilted. Use at least four pins – one per corner – or more if it is a large design. Using a darning foot, you can stitch over the tracing very accurately and easily. When you have finished, tear the paper away. Architects' detail paper is also good.

The stitching

Begin by quilting all the straight lines in the ditch, stitching on the low side of the seams which have been pressed to one side, making the quilting lines almost invisible. Use a walking foot and increase the stitch length a little, to 3 or 3.5 mm; tension is normal.

For small pieces, the work can be handled flat under the machine; for larger pieces or bed-sized quilts, roll the two opposite sides of the quilt towards the centre, leaving the area to be stitched exposed. Place the quilt under the machine and, beginning at the top edge of the centre row, stitch all the rows out to the right side of the quilt, unrolling it as you go. Turn the quilt and repeat for the other side. Now roll the other two sides and stitch at right angles to the first lot of quilting, again beginning at the centre top and working to one side, then turning and re-rolling to complete. Now, you should have stabilised areas in which you can work.

Use a darning foot and free machine-stitching to outline appliqués, stipple-quilt areas or 'draw' designs. Appliqués can be given extra definition by quilting in features and leg lines on creatures, or defining flower centres. In many cases, simply outlining appliqués will make them stand out, even making them look as if they are padded.

Stippling or Cornelli quilting is like doodling with a pencil on paper, where the lines never cross. Plan your stitching so that you have as few starts and stops as possible, and always try to leave yourself a pathway out as you stipple round your designs.

For free machine-quilting, you will probably have to adjust the tension to get a good stitch. Generally, this means loosening it a little but, on some machines, tightening the top tension gives a better result. Use a sample of two layers of fabric plus batting for testing.

MAKING A ROD POCKET

A rod pocket, finished to a minimum depth of 6.5 cm (2$1/2$ in) by the width of your quilt, is required if the quilt is to be hung.

Above: Machine-quilting in two designs adds interest to the plain areas.

Cut the fabric, preferably the same as the quilt backing fabric, the width of the quilt plus 3 cm (1 in) by 16 cm (6 in) deep. Turn in 2 cm (³/4 in) at each short end and hem the ends. Bring the two long sides together and sew a 1 cm (¹/2 in) seam. Fold the tube so the seam is on the outside at the centre back of the tube (against the quilt back) and pin the tube to the back of the quilt at approximately 1 cm (¹/2 in) below the top. Blindstitch across the top of the tube, so the tube seam is hidden between the quilt and the sleeve.

Roll the top fold of the sleeve up to the top of the quilt binding so it can't be seen from the front, and pin the resulting lower fold of the tube in place on the back. Blindstitch across this lower fold and up the side of the tube. This creates a gusset for the rod to sit in and your quilt will hang perfectly.

Above: The label on the Z Flower Quilt on page 73.

LABELLING YOUR QUILT

Every quilt deserves a label. Make the label special by appliquéing a small motif or two to match the quilt front. Add the name of the quilt, your name and the date and the name of the person for whom it was made or the occasion for which it was made. This information could be embroidered on the label or written on it with a permanent fabric marker.

FABRICS

Mainly cottons and some silks were used for the projects in this book. Almost any fabrics can be used with the Vliesofix method, although some fabrics need to be protected from the direct heat of the iron. Glad Bake is very useful for this purpose. Use a scrap piece of fabric to test that the iron is just hot

Above: The label on the Medieval Inspirations Quilt on page 16.

enough to fuse the Vliesofix to the fabric, but not so hot that it scorches.

For bed quilts or articles which will be washed, prewash the fabrics, then dry them in a dryer. This way you can test for colour fastness and also be sure fabrics will not shrink at different rates when washed later.

Once you begin the appliqué, you will probably find yourself looking at fabrics in a different light. One pattern might suggest leaves, another feathers or another one bricks. If you see a fabric you think will be useful then 25 cm (10 in) will make quite a few appliqués – 50 cm is even better.

You can very quickly become addicted to collecting fabrics, so it's best to be organised. Sort them into colours and types, and store them in labelled or clear plastic boxes so that you can find them easily.

THE SEWING MACHINE

Always make sure your machine is totally free of lint around the bobbin case. Clean it thoroughly before using it and after every few bobbins, especially when sewing through all the layers of Vliesofix and backings. Keep the sewing machine oiled according to the manufacturer's instructions.

Use an appliqué or clear plastic foot for satin stitching. An open-toed embroidery foot is also excellent so you can see your stitching clearly. Use a darning foot for embroidery. For attaching braid, a braiding foot, or for wider braids an open-toed embroidery foot, will help you guide the braid through.

A walking foot is excellent for straight or gently curved quilting lines. If your machine has a dial to adjust the pressure on the presser foot, then release the pressure a little for satin stitching, as it allows you more freedom of movement with your fabric.

THREADS

Best results are achieved by using machine-embroidery rayon threads, especially for the satin stitching. These will give you a smooth, even look with a lovely sheen, which you cannot get with polyester or cotton threads, although these can also be used, of course. There are many brands to choose from.

A number 40 thread is good and is the one most widely available. For a heavier look, a number 30 rayon embroidery thread can be used, or for some free machine-stitching which needs more definition, try Cotona 30, which is a cotton thread.

There is also a wide range of shiny, metallic threads available. The easiest to use are the smooth finish ones. These are excellent for highlights and for special effects.

In the bobbin, use Bobbinfil or a fine polyester or polycotton thread when appliquéing directly onto the background. Bobbinfil comes in either black or white. If your tension is set correctly, you should be able to use black with dark colours, white with light colours and not have it show on the top. Being very fine, (number 70), the Bobbinfil helps to give a smooth, even satin stitch with the rayon threads. If you have trouble with the bobbin thread showing on the top of your work, one solution is to use the same coloured thread in the bobbin as through the needle.

For the three-dimensional appliqués, it is best to use the same thread through the needle and in the bobbin, as the colour will then be even on all visible edges. When using rayon thread in the bobbin, wind the bobbin a little more slowly than usual so you do not stretch or break the thread.

COUCHING THREADS AND BRAIDS

Thicker threads or braids which will not go through the machine, such as those used in outlining on the panels, can be couched down. Use a braiding foot, or guide wider braids under an open-toed embroidery foot using a satay stick or something similar – instead of your fingers – to hold them in place as you stitch. With monofilament thread through the needle and a polyester thread in the bobbin, use a zigzag stitch about 1.5 mm (less than 1/16 in) long and 1.5 mm (less than 1/16 in) wide. Gold thread can be used through the needle to couch some of the finer threads.

Begin by knotting the thread to be couched underneath and bringing it up through the fabric with a tapestry needle. To finish, thread it through the tapestry needle again, pull the thread through to the back and knot it against the fabric.

Couched threads and fine braids can also be attached after the quilting is completed. To start, use a tapestry needle and insert the thread about 2.5 cm (1 in) away from where you will begin stitching. Leave a short tail of thread hanging out. To finish, thread the tapestry needle, insert the needle at the end of the last stitch and bring it out about 2.5 cm (1 in) away from the stitching. Cut the tails level with the top of the quilt and they will pull into the batting out of sight.

Heavy threads and braids, attached after quilting, need to have the raw ends doubled under or overlapped neatly and secured on the top of the quilt with invisible stitches. Have as few joins as possible.

NEEDLES

For all appliqué and machine-embroidery, it is best to use a Metalfil or System N needle, size 75 or 80. This needle has a bigger eye and helps to stop the thread breaking.

The needle should be sharp and the correct size for the thread and fabric – a size 80 needle is good for most work. Change the needle after every six to eight hours of stitching, or more often if it becomes blunt.

YOU WILL NEED

- 4.5 m (5 yd) of main fabric
- 1 m (1 yd) of fabric for the letters
- 30 cm (12 in) of various fabrics for the leaves
- at least 25 cm (10 in) each of about twelve coordinating fabrics for the appliqués
- 3 m (3¼ yd) of Vliesofix
- 3 m (3¼ yd) of iron-on stabiliser (Tearaway)
- 20 cm (8 in) of iron-on medium-weight Vilene
- 20 cm (8 in) of heat-vanishing muslin (Thermogaze)
- 4.5 cm (5 yd) of fabric for the backing
- full-size batting
- machine-embroidery rayon and metallic threads
- Bobbinfil (black and white) or fine poly-cotton or polyester for the bobbin
- polycotton or polyester thread to match the quilt back for machine-quilting
- monofilament thread for quilting and attaching braid
- 50 m (52 yd) of fine braid to edge all the blocks (optional)
- various coloured and dyed flat-backed rhinestones or beads for eyes and highlights
- gemstone glue
- thick gold thread for couching
- usual sewing supplies
- drawing and tracing materials

Medieval Inspirations Quilt

Finished size (after quilting):

170 cm x 210 cm (68 in x 83½ in)

The letters for this medieval quilt were derived from 15th and 16th century wood blocks, simplified a little to make them easier to appliqué (although there are still some tight corners). The D, G and I were totally changed to make them recognisable to modern eyes, but they are still in keeping with the medieval feel.

Instead of the alphabet being set out in conventional ABC order, this quilt is a 'hunt for the letter' affair. They are all there, interspersed with some purely pattern blocks and some border strips, taken from the letter block designs.

Although the blocks are of varying size, the actual letters are all the same height, 18 cm (7 in). This means they could be used in blocks of 25.5 cm (10 in) or 30.5 cm (12 in) very easily, to accommodate a more regular design.

The designs around the letters are inspired by the beautiful medieval tapestries and illuminated manuscript borders. Many medieval borders are incredibly intricate and ornate, depicting creatures and foliage of every conceivable design. Some creatures and flower shapes occur often throughout the period, others seem to be rather uncommon. The flowers and creatures on the quilt are representative of many examples. They could be changed from block to block, the designs enlarged or reduced, or used in different combinations on many projects.

There are five Australian motif designs, which are not found on any medieval manuscripts, of course. However, they fit very well in this context, particularly the lyre bird whose tail is very reminiscent of the peacock's tail, for design purposes.

For the appliqués, you will find you use three or four fabrics most frequently, but having twelve gives you the option of more variety. They can be cottons, silks, hand-dyed fabrics, prints or plains.

THE BLOCKS

See the individual block designs, templates and instructions on pages 22–53.

To make the quilt as it is, all the measurements are given on the quilt diagram on page 16. Follow the general instructions for techniques on pages 4–13 and the particular instructions that accompany each block. Remember, the block designs are given at half size and will need to be enlarged before they are traced.

THE BORDERS

Note: Complete as much work as possible on the borders before attaching them to the quilt centre, mitring the corners. Any three-dimensional and padded work is added after the borders are attached and the quilting is completed.

1   From the main fabric, cut two strips 16.5 cm x 228 cm (6½ in x 90 in) and two strips 16.5 cm x 190 cm (6½ in x 75 in). These measurements allow for mitred corners.

2   The top border has flowers from the Block 14 (S Block) and the Block 23 (E Block). Prepare and stitch these in the same way as for the blocks.

3   The left-hand border has the three left-hand side towers from Block 31 and the right-hand border has the three right-hand side towers. The towers are half as

1
26 cm x 26 cm
(10 in x 10 in)

2
26 cm x 26 cm
(10 in x 10 in)

36

3
26 cm x 26 cm
(10 in x 10 in)

4
26 cm x 26 cm
(10 in x 10 in)

5
26 cm x 26 cm
(10 in x 10 in)

6
13 cm x
36 cm
(5 in x
15 in)

7
18 cm x
36 cm
(6 1/2 in x
15 in)

8
26 cm x 31 cm
(10 in x 12 1/2 in)

9
26 cm x 26 cm
(10 in x 10 in)

35

10
26 cm x 31 cm
(10 in x 12 1/2 in)

11
21 cm x 36 cm
(7 1/2 in x 15 in)

12
31 cm x 26 cm
(12 1/2 in x 10 in)

13
26 cm x 31 cm
(10 in x 12 1/2 in)

14
26 cm x 26 cm
(10 in x 10 in)

15
26 cm x 26 cm
(10 in x 10 in)

33

16
21 cm x 26 cm
(7 1/2 in x 10 in)

32

17
31 cm x 26 cm
(12 1/2 in x 10 in)

18
26 cm x 31 cm
(10 in x 12 1/2 in)

19
26 cm x 26 cm
(10 in x 10 in)

21
26 cm x 26 cm
(10 in x 10 in)

23
26 cm x 31 cm
(10 in x 12 1/2 in)

20
26 cm x 30 cm
(10 in x 12 in)

22
26 cm x 26 cm
(10 in x 10 in)

25
26 cm x 26 cm
(10 in x 10 in)

26
31 cm x 26 cm
(12 1/2 in x 10 in)

34

24
26 cm x 26 cm
(10 in x 10 in)

27
26 cm x 26 cm
(10 in x 10 in)

37

28
26 cm x 26 cm
(10 in x 10 in)

29
26 cm x 31 cm
(10 in x 12 1/2 in)

30
26 cm x 31 cm
(10 in x 12 1/2 in)

31
26 cm x 26 cm
(10 in x 10 in)

Quilt Diagram

Block 32: 31 cm x 5 cm (12 1/2 in x 1 1/2 in)
Block 33: 5 cm x 31 cm (1 1/2 in x 12 1/2 in)
Block 34: 52 cm x 6 cm (21 in x 2 in)

Block 35: 5 cm x 31 cm (1 1/2 in x 12 1/2 in)
Block 36: 5 cm x 26 cm (1 1/2 in x 10 in)
Block 37: 5 cm x 26 cm (1 1/2 in x 10 in)

big again as on the original block. Prepare and stitch in the same way. Place flowers and leaves at the base of the towers.

4 The design in the centre of the bottom border is taken from the Block 19 (A Block). The hare and the hound are taken from Block 20 (H Block).

5 Extra flower and leaf motifs have been taken from Block 2 (Z Block), Block 12 (X Block), Block 14 (S Block), Block 19 (A Block) and Block 25 (C Block). More or less appliqués can be added to suit your personal taste.

6 The flowers from Block 18 have been made separately and stand away from the quilt (see page 5).

7 The dragon from Block 10 (D Block), the brolga from Block 24 (B Block) and the wren from Block 17 (W Block) have been made separately and padded as they were attached to the quilt (see page 6).

8 The dragonflies from Block 3 (V Block), and the bees, butterflies and snails (see the patterns for these on page 53) are made with three-dimensional appliqué (see page 5). The bees and dragonflies use heat-vanishing muslin for the wings (see page 9).

CONSTRUCTION

Note: Assemble the quilt, following the quilt diagram and the construction diagrams on pages 18-19.

1 From the sashing fabric, cut strips 4 cm (1¹/2 in) wide.

2 Join Block 1, Block 2 and Block 36 (Fig. 1). Set aside.

3 Join Block 6, Block 7, Block 12, Block 32 and Block 17 (Fig. 2). Set aside.

4 Join Block 8, Block 13 and Block 18 (Fig. 3).

5 Join the sets made in steps 3 and 4 together, side by side, then join the set made in step 2 to the top (Fig. 4).

6 Join Block 25 and Block 26 (Fig. 5). Set aside.

7 Join Block 27, Block 37 and Block 28 (Fig. 6).

8 Join the sets made in steps 6 and 7, then

join that to the bottom of the large section already joined (Fig. 7).

9 Join Block 3, Block 9, Block 14, Block 19 and Block 20 in one long strip (Fig. 8). Set aside.

10 Join Block 4 to Block 5 (Fig. 9). Set aside.

11 Join Block 35 and Block 10. Join a length of sashing to the bottom, then join Block 33 to the bottom right-hand corner (Fig. 10). This will be an odd-shaped set.

12 Join Block 11 to Block 16 (Fig. 11).

13 Join the sets made in steps 11 and 12 (Fig. 12).

14 Join the set made in step 10 to the top of the set made in step 13 (Fig. 13).

15 Join Block 23, Block 24 and Block 31 (Fig. 14), then join this set to the bottom of the set made in step 14. Join a length of sashing to the left hand edge of Blocks 33, 23, 24 and 31.

16 Join Block 15, Block 21 and Block 22 (Fig. 15), then join this set to the large set made in step 15 (Fig. 16).

17 Join Block 29 and Block 30, then join Block 34 to the top (Fig. 17). Join a length of sashing to the top of this set. Set aside.

18 Join the long strip made in step 9 to the side of the large set of blocks made in step 16 (Fig. 18). The bottom of Block 20 should be level with the bottom of Block 22.

19 Join the set made in step 17 to the bottom of blocks 20 and 22, fitting the top right-hand corner squarely against Block 24 (Fig. 19).

20 Join the two large sections of the quilt top together with a length of sashing in between.

21 Join a length of sashing to all four sides of the quilt top.

22 Attach the appliquéd borders to the quilt top, mitring the corners.

Above: Detail of the appliquéd flowers on the quilt border.

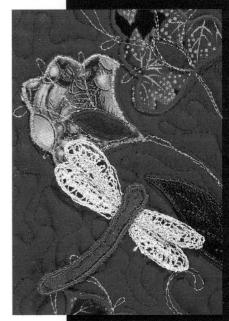

Above: Detail of a dragonfly on the quilt border.

QUILTING

1 Pin the three layers of quilt together following the instructions for machine-quilting on page 10.

2 Using a walking foot, first complete all the straight line quilting, in the ditch, outlining all the blocks.

3 Quilt the blocks with the free machine-stitching technique, outlining the appliqués and filling any spaces with stipple quilting. See the instructions for free machine-stitching and stipple quilting on pages 8–11.

TO FINISH

1 Cut 6 cm (1 1/2 in) wide binding and attach it to the front of the quilt, mitring the corners. Turn the binding to the back of the quilt and slipstitch it in place by hand.

2 Couch the braid on, following the instructions for couching on page 13.

3 Attach the three-dimensional and padded pieces, following the instructions on pages 5–6.

4 Stitch on a rod pocket, following the instructions on page 11.

Label your quilt and it is finished!

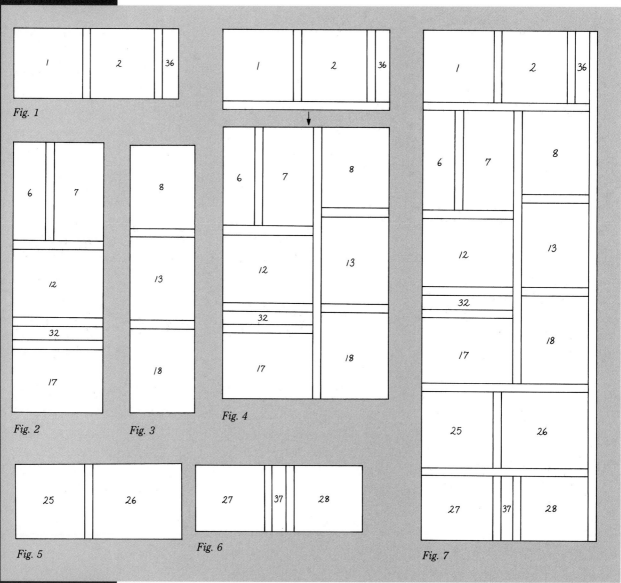

Fig. 1

Fig. 2   *Fig. 3*

Fig. 4

Fig. 5

Fig. 6

Fig. 7

Above and right: Construction Diagrams

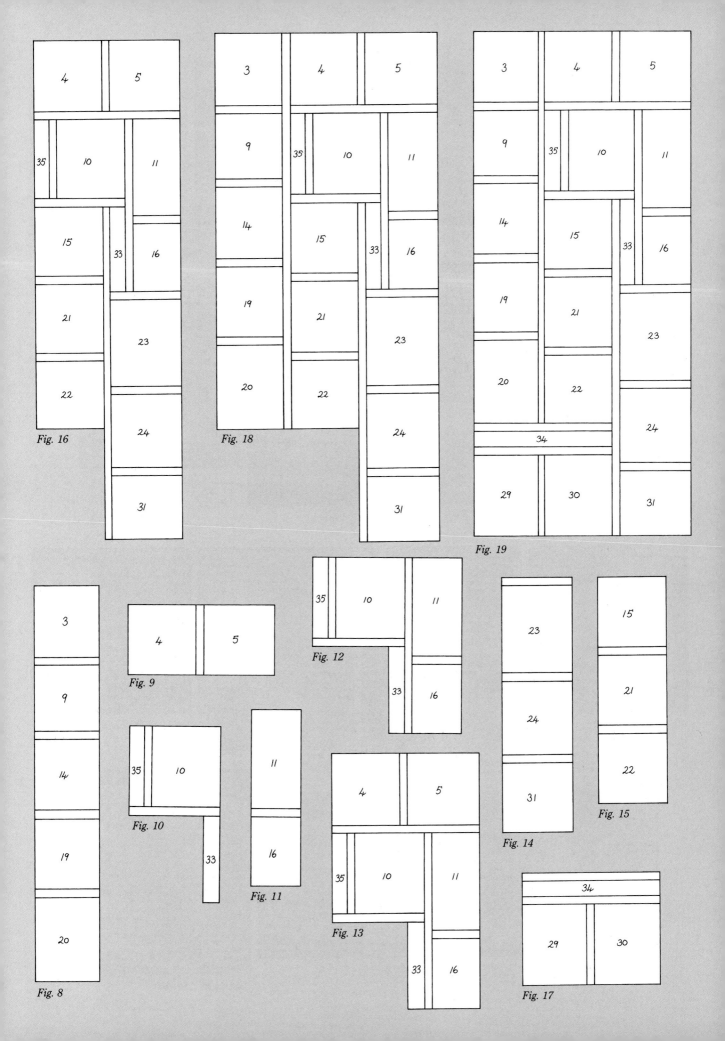

Fig. 16

Fig. 18

Fig. 19

Fig. 9

Fig. 12

Fig. 14

Fig. 15

Fig. 8

Fig. 10

Fig. 11

Fig. 13

Fig. 17

Block 19 (A Block)

Block 24 (B Block)

Block 25 (C Block)

Block 10 (D Block)

Block 6 (I Block)

Block 11 (J Block)

Block 13 (K Block)

Block 9 (L block)

Block 27 (P Block)

Block 30 (Q Block)

Block 8 (R Block)

Block 14 (S Block)

Block 17 (W Block)

Block 12 (X Block)

Block 29 (Y Block)

Block 23 (E Block)

Block 4 (F Block)

Block 15 (G Block)

Block 20 (H Block)

Block 26 (M Block)

Block 22 (N Block)

Block 28 (O Block)

Block 5 (T Block)

Block 1 (U Block)

Block 3 (V Block)

Block 2 (Z Block)

Block 7 (Adapted)

Block 18 (Adapted)

Block 21 (Adapted)

BLOCK 1 (U BLOCK)
26 cm x 26 cm (10 in x 10 in)

The most famous unicorns are possibly in the 'Lady and the Unicorn' tapestries, and they definitely belong with dragons, gryphons and other mythical creatures. The shape of the flowers and leaves seemed to fit with the unicorn.

1   Cut out the background and appliqué pieces. Prepare them as instructed on pages 4–13.

2   Arrange the unicorn leaping through the letter, leaving space at the top left and the bottom right for the flowers. Fuse, then satin stitch the unicorn and the letter in place. Use silver thread for the unicorn to add to the mythical feel. Use free machine-embroidery for the mane and tail, but satin stitch the horn as it gives a better shape.

3   Arrange the flowers and leaves. Fuse them in place, then satin stitch. Use free machine-stitching to embellish the flowers and for the stems.

4   Add one medium-sized rhinestone with a tiny one beside it for the eye.

BLOCK 2 (Z BLOCK)
26 cm x 26 cm (10 in x 10 in)

This motif was adapted from one of the wood-block designs. It is a particularly good one to adapt for all sorts of uses. The small border design is from a manuscript border.

1 Cut out the background and appliqué pieces. Prepare them as instructed on pages 4–13.

2 Centre the letter, leaves and the flowers on the block. Fuse them in place, then satin stitch.

3 Free machine-stitch the stems and scrolls. Embellish the flowers with free machine-stitching.

4 Arrange the border flowers and leaves. Fuse them in place, then satin stitch. Use free machine-stitching for the stems.

5 Couch thick gold thread down, using gold metallic thread through the needle and following the couching instructions on page 13.

BLOCK 3 (V BLOCK)
26 cm x 26 cm (10 in x 10 in)

Violets are often depicted in borders – for example, the Soane *Books of Hours*, from the late 15th century or the Letter D in a French *Book of Hours* from the late 14th century. There are also many small creatures such as dragonflies, snails or bees in manuscript border illustrations.

1 Cut out the background and the various appliqué pieces. Prepare them as instructed on pages 4–13.

2 Arrange the letter in the centre of the block, then add the violets and leaves which form a circular design, leaving space at the four corners for the dragonflies. Fuse them in place. Satin stitch the violets, including the stems.

3 Arrange the dragonflies in the corners of the block. Fuse them in place, then satin stitch the wings and the bodies.

4 Use free machine-stitching to embellish the violets and the veins on the leaves. Use the same stitching technique on the wings of the dragonflies.

BLOCK 4 (F BLOCK)

26 cm x 26 cm (10 in x 10 in)

The fish is very symbolical and formed an appropriate enrichment for the walls of a baptistery. Though a recognisable shape, this fish has a definite medieval feel.

1 Cut the background and appliqué pieces. Prepare them as instructed on page 4–13.

2 With a dressmaker's pencil, water-soluble pen or something similar, mark where the seaweed fronds cross over and under one another. Mark the lines defining the stones.

3 Satin stitch the appliqués and the line details. The fins and tail of the fish also have lines of free machine-embroidery to define their shape.

4 Add a blue or clear flat-backed rhinestone for the eye.

BLOCK 5 (T BLOCK)
26 cm x 26 cm (10 in x 10 in)

These decorative beasts came from a Gothic border illustration. The tails waved right round the border forming their own design. The flower shapes echo the spiky leaves.

1 Cut out the background and appliqué pieces. Prepare them as instructed on pages 4–13.

2 Arrange the letter and the beasts so they are centred on the block, twining the necks around the letter. Fuse them in place, then satin stitch the beasts in silver thread and the letter in gold thread.

3 Arrange the flowers and leaves. Fuse them in place, then satin stitch. Embellish the flowers and stitch the stems and swirls with free machine-embroidery.

4 Add two shiny flat-backed rhinestones for the eyes.

BLOCK 6 (I BLOCK)
13 cm x 36 cm (5 in x 15 in)

In the Book of Kells, there are many snakes, most with heads like ducks and often tails like fish. This one is rather snakelike, but could be made more fanciful by altering the head. The border has very stylised leaves.

1 Cut out the background and appliqué pieces. Prepare them as instructed on pages 4–13.

2 Arrange the letter in the centre of the block with the snake twined around it. Fuse them in place, then satin stitch around the edges.

3 Mark in the border, then arrange the leaves. Fuse them in position, then satin stitch.

4 Couch the border line with thick gold thread, using gold metallic thread through the needle and following the couching instructions on page 13.

BLOCK 7
ADAPTED BLOCK

18 cm x 36 cm (6¹/2 in x 15 in)

Here Block 19 (A Block) has been reversed, then part of the design element is added to each side. This design was also used for the bolster on page 77. It would make an excellent design to fill a square by repeating the design four times.

BLOCK 8 (R BLOCK)
26 cm x 31 cm (10 in x 12¹/₂ in)

The 'Lady and the Unicorn' tapestries (1490–1500) in the Musée de Cluny in Paris have some of the best known rabbit motifs. These rabbits are so lifelike, and they make a wonderful design. The flower shapes are common to many designs and borders.

1 Cut out the background and appliqué pieces. Prepare them as instructed on pages 4–13.

2 Arrange the rabbits so they fit under the letter, leaving equal spaces at the sides for the flowers. Fuse, then satin stitch the letter and rabbits.

3 Arrange the flowers and leaves above the rabbits and around the letter. The design is partially symmetrical with the central flowers twining through the R. Embellish with free-machine embroidery.

4 Embroider the rabbits' whiskers. Add oval flat-backed rhinestones for the eyes.

BLOCK 9 (L BLOCK)
26 cm x 26 cm (10 in x 10 in)

This block features the lyre bird with its beautiful tail and ability to mimic every sound it hears.

1   Cut out the background and appliqué pieces. Prepare them as instructed on pages 4–13.
2   Position the lyre bird so that it stands on the letter L. Satin stitch around the letter and the bird's body. Satin stitch the four main tail feathers, before embroidering the tail.

3   The darkish grey feathers at the base of the tail are embroidered first. Draw the centre of the feathers on the background as a guide for stitching. There are twelve of these filament feathers. Begin at the base and stitch to the feather tip. Working back down to the base, stitch the fine filaments of the feathers on either side of the central line, backtracking a little each time on the centre line to make it stand out sufficiently.
4   The flowers are leschenaultia, a beautiful flower from Western Australia. Satin stitch the flowers and machine-embroider the fine leaves and the flower centres.

BLOCK 10 (D BLOCK)

26 cm x 31 cm (10 in x 12¹/₂ in)

It would not be a medieval quilt without a dragon. This dragon is derived from *Très Riches Heures du Duc de Berry*, illuminated by the Limburg brothers between about 1411 and 1416.

Note: For a metric block, place the dragon and the letter, then arrange the foliage to fit.

1 Cut out the background and appliqué pieces. Prepare them as instructed on pages 4–13. Use silk for the wings and front of the dragon.

2 First arrange the letter and the dragon on the background, then fuse them in place. Arrange the foliage to fill in the spaces and fuse them in place.

3 Satin stitching the appliqué with gold thread gives life to the whole design. Satin stitch the markings on the wings. Later, when the quilting in monofilament thread is added, it should be worked very close to this satin stitching to make the wings stand out.

4 Free machine-stitch the scales on the front of the dragon and the stems of the foliage.

5 Add a red, flat-backed rhinestone for the dragon's eye.

BLOCK 11 (J BLOCK)

21 cm x 36 cm (7¹/2 in x 15 in)

These creatures are from a lectern Bible from the mid-1400s. They make an excellent design element and can also be joined by their tails as in the border on Bryce's Quilt on page 64. This is another leaf design border with couched gold thread.

1   Cut out the background and appliqué pieces. Prepare them as instructed on pages 4–13.

2   Arrange the two creatures with their necks entwined in the centre of the block. The letter sits over the top. Fuse them in place, then satin stitch.

3   Mark in the border. Arrange the leaf design and fuse it in place. Satin stitch. Use free machine-embroidery for the stems.

4   Couch the border line with thick gold thread, using gold metallic thread through the needle and following the couching instructions on page 13.

5   Add clear flat-backed rhinestones for the eyes.

BLOCK 12 (X BLOCK)
31 cm x 26 cm (12½ in x 10 in)

There are many stylised medieval tree designs, some with fruit such as in the *St Louis Psalter* of 1253. This beautiful one was adapted from the *Hours of Giangaleazzo* begun in 1388.

1   Cut out the background and appliqué pieces. Prepare them as instructed on pages 4–13.

2   Centre the letter and tree on the block with the cross of the X just above the top of the trunk. Fuse them in place, then satin stitch.

3   The leaves underneath are satin stitched and embellished with free machine-embroidery.

4   Stitch the fruit and leaf borders, including the stems, on either side with free machine-stitching.

5   Couch thick gold thread down, using gold metallic thread through the needle and following the couching instructions on page 13.

BLOCK 13 (K BLOCK)
26 cm x 31 cm (10 in x 12¹/2 in)

The kookaburra is one of the best known Australian birds. Its uncanny laugh would surely have put it with some of the strange medieval creatures. The flowers on the block are snow daisies from the Australian alpine regions. The leaves in particular are very medieval-looking.

Note: For a metric block, place the kooka-burra and the letter, then bring the top and bottom borders in a little closer to fit.

1 Cut out the background and appliqué pieces. Prepare them as instructed on pages 4–13.
2 Arrange the kookaburras and the letter in the centre of the block. Satin stitch the letter and birds.
3 Arrange the flowers and leaves and fuse them in position. Satin stitch the leaves. Use free machine-embroidery to stitch the flowers, outlining their many petals.
4 Couch the border line with thick gold thread, using gold metallic thread through the needle and following the couching instructions on page 13.

BLOCK 14 (S BLOCK)
26 cm x 26 cm (10 in x 10 in)

Hunting scenes were a very popular subject. This stag was illustrated in a manuscript, dating from 1450. The strawberries are from a gospel lectionary from the Netherlands.

1   Cut out the background and appliqué pieces. Prepare them as instructed on pages 4–13.

2   Arrange the letter and the stag so there is space to the left and underneath for the flowers. Fuse them in place, then satin stitch. Define the stag's legs with satin stitching.

3   Arrange the strawberries, flowers and leaves. Fuse them in place, then satin stitch. Use free machine-stitching to embellish the flowers and for the stems.

4   Add a flat-backed rhinestone for the eye.

BLOCK 15 (G BLOCK)
26 cm x 26 cm (10 in x 10 in)

Another mythical creature, the gryphon or griffin, features in many medieval illustrations. A *Book of Hours* from Paris in the early 15th century has one like this, with a knotted neck. The acanthus-type foliage surrounds it.

1 Cut out the background and appliqué pieces. Prepare them as instructed on pages 4–13. Use silk for the wings to make them stand out.

2 Because the gryphon has leaves in his mouth and he is intertwined with the letter, it is best to arrange the whole block on the background, before fusing the pieces into place.

3 Draw clear guidelines around the knotted neck and for the wing markings to make the stitching easier. Most of the block is satin stitched. The leaves are highlighted with embroidery. Add a few curls and swirls to fill in the spaces.

4 Add a bright flat-backed rhinestone for the eye.

BLOCK 16
ADAPTED BLOCK
21 cm x 26 cm (7¹/₂ in x 10 in)

Block 22 (N Block) is reproduced almost exactly, only the centre flower added. Enlarged as one continuous row, this would make a beautiful border.

Embellish each large flower with free machine-embroidery and add more swirling lines to fill the spaces.

BLOCK 17 (W BLOCK)
31 cm x 26 cm (12¹/2 in x 10 in)

Australian superb blue wrens are well known and easily identified because of the beautiful colouring on the males. They are common in southern and eastern Australia. The flower is a royal bluebell, also from southern and eastern Australia and the floral emblem of the Australian Capital Territory.

1 Cut out the background and appliqué pieces. Prepare them as instructed on pages 4–13.
2 Centre the letter on the block and arrange the two wrens sitting on it. The wren pieces are quite small, so take care to arrange the appropriate underlaps. Free machine-stitch the beaks and feet, and satin stitch the rest of the birds.
3 Arrange the flowers, buds and leaves around the border, then satin stitch them. Free machine-stitch the stems and the embellishments on the flowers.
4 Add flat-backed rhinestones for the eyes.

BLOCK 18
ADAPTED BLOCK

26 cm x 31 cm (10 in x 12½ in) panel.

The bird was inspired by an early 15th century French manuscript; the shapes of the leaves and flowers are common to many designs. The design stands alone, or you could take some of the elements and redesign it.

To make the block as it is:

1 Begin by placing the bird with its head a little more than halfway down the block. Arrange the foliage around it. Fuse it in place, then satin stitch.

2 Free machine-stitch the bird's legs, the stems and the flower embellishments.

3 Add a flat-backed rhinestone for the eye.

BLOCK 19 (A BLOCK)
26 cm x 26 cm (10 in x 10 in)

Part of a design on what was probably an altar frontal about 1470–1500. The border is one of the many leaf designs.

1 Cut out the background and appliqué pieces. Prepare them as instructed on pages 4–13.

2 Use satin stitch for the appliqué and enhance with free machine-embroidery, using the block design as a guide.

3 Couch the gold line with thick gold thread, using gold metallic thread through the needle and following the couching instructions on page 13.

BLOCK 20 (H BLOCK)
26 cm x 30 cm (10 in x 12 in)

This hounds and hares design dates back to about 1370, when they appear in the border of a manuscript on the history of Rome.

Note: For a metric block, bring in the top and bottom borders to fit.

1   Cut out the background and appliqué pieces. Prepare them as instructed on pages 4–13.

2   The letter, hound, hare, trees and ornamental stands are all satin stitched. The ivy leaves are very small. After backing them with Vliesofix, fuse them to the background and appliqué them by free machine-stitching over them. The free machine-stitching is also used to create the branches which join the leaves together.

3   Use tiny flat-backed rhinestones for the eyes or embroider the eyes with a French knot.

BLOCK 21
ADAPTED BLOCK
26 cm x 26 cm (10 in x 10 in) panel.

Note: For a metric block, bring in the top and bottom borders to fit.

This panel was adapted from Block 2 (Z Block). This design has many possibilities, created simply by rearranging the centre leaves. One slight variation has been used in the Flower Quilt on page 73.

BLOCK 22 (N BLOCK)

26 cm x 26 cm (10 in x 10 in)

These flowers are also from a Spanish *Book of Hours* which dates from the second half of the 15th century.

1 Cut out the background and appliqué pieces. Prepare them as instructed on pages 4–13.

2 Arrange the letter in the centre of the block. Fuse it in place, then satin stitch.

3 Arrange the flowers and leaves, then fuse them in place. The flowers and leaves are satin-stitched. Free machine-embroider the stems and the embellishments on the flowers.

BLOCK 23 (E BLOCK)
26 cm x 31 cm (10 in x 12¹/₂ in)

Note: For a metric block, place the eagle and the letter, then arrange the flowers and leaves to fit.

1 Cut out the background and appliqué pieces. The wing and the rest of the eagle are cut out in one piece. Prepare them as instructed on pages 4–13.

2 First, arrange the letter and the eagle on the block background, then fuse them in place.

3 The wing shape and feathers are defined with satin stitching.

4 Stylised flowers make a beautiful design, especially embellished with gold embroidery. Arrange the flowers and leaves in a pleasing way around the block, then fuse them in place.

5 Add a black flat-backed rhinestone for the eye.

BLOCK 24 (B BLOCK)
26 cm x 26 cm (10 in x 10 in)

This block features the Australian brolga, a tall stately bird renowned for its elegant and elaborate dancing. The flowers are those of the spotted gum.

1 Cut out the background and appliqué pieces. Prepare them as instructed on pages 4–13.
2 Weave the brolga round the letter as shown in the diagram. Satin stitch the appliqués. Use satin stitch to define the wing markings and a very narrow satin stitch (approximately 1.5) to define the beak and legs.
3 To embroider the gum blossom using silver thread, first make a small circle, then radiate the blossom shape around it. Change to creamy white rayon thread and embroider over the silver colour, letting the silver show through. Clear seed beads can be stitched at intervals round the edges of the gum blossom flower to add sparkle.
4 Couch gold thread down the side of the gum blossom border, using gold metallic thread through the needle and following the couching instructions on page 13.

BLOCK 25 (C BLOCK)
26 cm x 26 cm (10 in x 10 in)

Castles appear in many manuscripts, usually forming part of the background. For example, in the fictional *Travels of Sir John Mandeville*, an early 15th century illumination, there are very elaborate houses, castles and towers.

1 Cut out the background and appliqué pieces. Prepare them as instructed on pages 4–13. When cutting this block, be sure to leave underlaps on the various castle sections.

2 Fuse the letter, main castle pieces, flowers and leaves in place on the background, then satin stitch around the edges of all the pieces.

3 Fuse the flags, windows, etc in place. These can then be stitched on with free machine-stitching.

4 The flowers are embellished with embroidery, with either beads or rhinestones in the centres. The stems are free machine-stitched.

BLOCK 26 (M BLOCK)
31 cm x 26 cm (12¹/₂ in x 10 in)

There are monkeys, including monkeys with human heads, found in medieval illustrations.

Note: For a metric block, place the monkey and the letter, then adjust the position of the appliqués at the sides to fit.

1 Cut out the background and appliqué pieces. Prepare them as instructed on pages 4–13.

2 Arrange the monkey and the letter in the centre of the block. Fuse them in place, then satin stitch.

3 Arrange the flower border and fuse it in place. Satin stitch the leaves and flowers. Use free machine-embroidery to make the swirling lines in between.

4 Couch the diamond shape with thick gold thread, using gold metallic thread through the needle and following the couching instructions on page 13.

5 Add flat-backed rhinestones for the eyes.

BLOCK 27 (P BLOCK)
26 cm x 26 cm (10 in x 10 in)

This is a peacock from the *Book of Kells*. There are many birds and creatures included in the lines of text.

1 Cut out the background and appliqué pieces. Prepare them as instructed on pages 4–13.

2 Arrange the letter and the peacock in the centre of the block and fuse them in place. Satin stitch the peacock. Work the crest with free machine-embroidery.

3 Satin stitch the flowers in the border. The rest of the design is free machine-stitched. The stems of the flowers and buds form the linear border design.

BLOCK 28 (O BLOCK)
26 cm x 26 cm (10 in x 10 in)

There are many owls to be found in
manuscript borders and *Books of Hours*,
some with human faces, but this one is an
Australian powerful owl.

1   Cut out the background and appliqué
    pieces. Prepare them as instructed on
    pages 4–13. Cut out the owl all in
    one piece.
2   Arrange the letter and the owl on the
    block background. Fuse them in place,
    then satin stitch. Define the wings and
    feathers with satin stitching. Satin stitch
    the beak and the feet.
3   The blossoms are *Eucalyptus ficifolia* and
    they are stitched with free machine-
    stitching. Using gold thread, first make a
    small circle, then radiate the blossom
    shape around it. Change to red rayon
    thread and embroider over the gold,
    allowing some of the gold to show
    through. Clear or red seed beads can be
    stitched at intervals around the edge of
    the blossom to add sparkle.
4   Satin stitch the leaves and gumnuts.
5   Add two black, flat-backed rhinestones
    for the eyes.

BLOCK 29 (Y BLOCK)
26 cm x 31 cm (10 in x 12¹/₂ in)

This letter is very ornate. It has been simplified on the quilt on page 64. The corner scrolls are of Gothic origin.

Note: For a metric block, adjust the position of the corner scrolls to fit.

1 Cut out the background and appliqué pieces. Prepare them as instructed on pages 4–13.

2 First arrange the corner scrolls on the block. Fuse them in place, then satin stitch.

3 Centre the letter and the flowers inside the scrolls. Fuse them in place, then satin stitch the edges.

4 Embellish the flowers with free machine-embroidery.

5 Couch the gold thread in a square, using gold metallic thread through the needle and following the couching instructions on page 13.

BLOCK 30 (Q BLOCK)
26 cm x 31 cm (10 in x 12¹/₂ in)

Many manuscripts have fine border designs based on ivy or other creeping vines. This one is similar to a Paris *Books of Hours* from the second quarter of the 15th century.

Note: For a metric block, place the quail and the letter, then adjust the position of the vine at the top and bottom to fit.

1   Cut out the background and appliqué pieces. Prepare them as instructed on pages 4–13.
2   First, arrange the letter and the quail on the block, then add the larger pieces including the large leaves. Fuse them in place, then satin stitch. Use satin stitch to define the feathers on the quail's wing.
3   Mark the position of the stems, then free machine-stitch the stems. Free machine-stitch the small leaves.

BLOCK 31
ADAPTED BLOCK
26 cm x 26 cm (10 in x 10 in) block.

This is the castle from Block 25
(C Block), but with a few additions. This
castle was also used in the quilt on page 64,
both whole and in part.

Arrange the castle a little above the
centre of the block with the flowers
underneath it. Fuse them in place, then
satin stitch.

THE NARROW BLOCKS

These filler blocks use motifs and borders from other blocks in the quilt. Simply trace the required elements and arrange them on the background to suit.

BLOCK 32

31 cm x 5 cm (12½ in x 1½ in)

This is the border design from Block 11 (J Block). Prepare and stitch in the same way as the main block.

BLOCK 33

5 cm x 31 cm (1½ in x 12½ in)

The flowers and leaves are taken from Block 23 (E Block). Prepare and stitch in the same way as for the main block.

BLOCK 34

52 cm x 6 cm (21 in x 2 in)

The hare and hounds are taken from Block 20 (H Block). The flowers and leaves are taken from Block 14 (S Block). Prepare and stitch in the same way as for the main blocks.

BLOCK 35

5 cm x 31 cm (1½ in x 12½ in)

This is taken from the border of Block 12 (X Block). Prepare and stitch in the same way as the main block.

BLOCK 36

5 cm x 26 cm (1½ in x 10 in)

This is taken from the border of Block 27 (P Block). Prepare and stitch in the same way as the main block.

BLOCK 37

5 cm x 26 cm (1½ in x 10 in)

This is taken from the border of Block 2 (Z Block). Prepare and stitch in the same way as the main block.

Border Designs

See Laura's Quilt on page 60.

Welcome

For something quite different, this folding screen can stand on a table or a chest in the hallway to welcome guests to your home. It can be made as photographed with WELCOME inside it, or perhaps you would prefer the family name or one person's name in the centre. The centre panel could also have a motif or design with no lettering at all.

Finished size (of the appliqué panels):
25 cm (10 in) square and 25 cm x 51 cm (10 in x 20 in).

CUTTING

From the background fabric, cut two pieces each 33 cm (13 in) square and one piece 33 cm x 61 cm (13 in x 24 in). Because they will be stretched, design the appliqués for the side panels to fit inside a 24 cm (9 1/2 in) square and for the centre panel to fit inside a space 24 cm x 49.5 cm (9 1/2 in x 19 1/2 in). This way the appliqué will not disappear over the edge of the frame. Mark these sizes on the fabric. Basting thread is a good way to mark, as it is easy to see and pulls out easily later.

APPLIQUE

See the patterns on pages 30 and 59 and the alphabet on the Pull Out Pattern Sheet.
Note: The lyre birds are the same size as in Block 9 (L Block) in the Medieval Inspirations Quilt. You will need one lyre bird facing left and one facing right.
1 Following the instructions for using Vliesofix on page 4, trace and cut out the required letters, leaves and lyre bird pieces. Fuse the Vliesofix to the backs of the appliqué fabrics. Cut them out.
2 Arrange the letters in a pleasing interlocking design and fuse them in position. They are approximately 6 cm (2 1/4 in) in from the marked edges all

round. Back the work with iron-on stabiliser. Satin stitch with gold thread.
3 Arrange the gum leaves around the border leaving space for embroidered flowers in groups of three. Satin stitch the leaves and free machine-embroider the vein lines on them.
4 Embroider the gum blossoms following the instructions for Block 28 (O Block) on page 49. Use gold thread first, then red thread over the top.

For the lyre birds
1 On the heat-vanishing muslin, trace the twelve filament feathers for the lyre bird's tail. You will need two sets of feathers, one facing left and the other facing right.
2 Put one tail into an 18 cm (7 in) spring hoop. Using white rayon machine-embroidery thread through the needle and the bobbin, and referring to the instructions for using heat-vanishing muslin on page 9, embroider the tail feathers. All the lines of stitching must connect to one another. Begin at the base of the feather and stitch in a gentle curve to the tip. As you stitch back to the base, stitch feather shapes on either side of this central line, making sure they

YOU WILL NEED
- [ ] I m (I yd) of fabric for the background
- [ ] 12 cm (5 in) of fabric for the letters and some leaves
- [ ] 10 cm (4 in) of a second green fabric for the leaves
- [ ] 40 cm (16 in) of fabric for the outside cover and lyre birds' bodies
- [ ] small pieces of light and dark grey fabrics for the lyre birds' tails
- [ ] small pieces of black fabric for the legs and beaks
- [ ] small pieces of multicoloured fabric for the long tail feathers
- [ ] 25 cm (10 in) of Vliesofix
- [ ] 30 cm (12 in) of iron-on stabiliser (Tearaway)
- [ ] 40 cm (16 in) of iron-on Pellon
- [ ] two black flat-backed rhinestones for the eyes
- [ ] gemstone glue
- [ ] one packet of heat-vanishing muslin (Thermogaze)
- [ ] Glad Bake
- [ ] embroidery hoop for the sewing machine – an 18 cm (7 in) spring hoop is ideal
Continued page 58

Left: The lyre bird's tail is stitched on heat-vanishing muslin.

- **machine-embroidery rayon threads: brown, black, green, grey, red, white**
- **metallic threads: gold, silver**
- **monofilament thread**
- **usual sewing supplies**
- **drawing and tracing materials**

For the frame
- **two art stretchers 51 cm (20 in) long (available from art supply shops)**
- **ten art stretchers 25.5 cm (10 in) long**
- **six 19 mm (³/4 in) pine drawer knobs for feet**
- **four small brass hinges**
- **two small brass knobs**
- **two small brass ornaments (optional)**
- **staples or small tacks**
- **four 1 m (1 yd) long strips of upholstery nails**
- **4 m (4¹/2 yd) of braid for the outside**
- **4 m (4¹/2 yd) of 19 mm (³/4 in) wide ribbon (optional)**
- **craft glue**
- **medium-weight card**

Note: You will also need a planer, a drill with a 19 mm (³/4 in) bit, a screwdriver, a hammer and sandpaper.

connect across. Again, stitch in a gentle curve to the tip of the feather and back to the base, thus creating the more solid line in the centre of the feather. Repeat this procedure for the twelve filament feathers. You will find you do not need as much stitching at the base of the tail feathers as all the feathers overlap. However, stitch enough to hold it all together. Complete the second bird's tail feathers.

3 Cut away most of the heat-vanishing muslin that has no stitching on it. Put the tail feathers between two pieces of Glad Bake and iron it until the muslin turns brown. Brush away the powder.

4 Arrange the two sets of lyre bird pieces on the two side panel backgrounds, making sure they form a good mirror image of each other. The four solid tail feathers, two light grey and two multicoloured, lie underneath the embroidered tail feathers. Having put everything in place, carefully lift off the embroidery and also the small, dark grey feather piece. These will be attached at a later stage. Tuck a small piece of Glad Bake under the lyre bird body where the dark grey feather piece was removed and fuse the pieces in place. The Glad Bake will prevent that part of the body being fused, enabling the dark grey feathers to be put in place later. Back the work with iron-on stabiliser, keeping the Glad Bake in place.

5 Satin stitch the leaves, lyre birds' bodies (leaving space to re-insert the tail), four solid feathers and the ornamental stand. Use free machine-embroidery to attach the beaks and legs.

6 When the stitching is completed, remove the Glad Bake and return the dark grey feathers and the embroidered tail feathers to their correct positions, with the ends of the embroidered feathers under the grey appliqué piece. Fill in the satin stitching gap on the body. Using grey thread, attach the grey tail feathers. Change to monofilament thread. Stitch from the base of each embroidered

feather to the tip and back again leaving the feathery pieces free on either side.

7 Remove the iron-on stabiliser from the back of the work and replace it with the iron-on Pellon.

QUILTING

1 Using free machine-stitching and monofilament thread, outline-quilt all the letters and motifs, adding a few extra quilting lines to the blossoms. Stitch again from the base to the tip of each feather and add a few curls and swirls around the leaves.

2 Attach the eyes using the gemstone glue.

THE BACK

1 Cut the fabric for the back: one piece 26.5 cm x 52 cm (10¹/2 in x 20¹/2 in) and two pieces 26.5 cm (10¹/2 in) square. Using white rayon embroidery thread on top and in the bobbin, embroider two small tails on the heat-vanishing muslin.

2 Stabilise the back of each 26.5 cm (10¹/2 in). Centre the design and appliqué the ornamental stand, tucking the ends of the tail feathers under the top of it. Free machine-stitch the tail in place.

TO CONSTRUCT THE FRAME

1 Begin by putting the art stretchers together. Four of the 25.5 cm (10 in) long stretchers go together for each side panel. The two 51 cm (20 cm) and the last two smaller ones make the centre panel. Fit them together so that they are as square as possible. Glue will hold them in place, though they can be so stiff that glue may not be necessary.

2 Smooth off all the corners with the sandpaper. Because the nail strips will take up space between the end panels when the frame is closed, you need to plane 3 mm (¹/8 in) off each centre edge making a gap of 6 mm (¹/4 in). The frame will then close easily, when it is all assembled.

3 Mark the places for the hinge screws

and make small holes, but do not finally attach the hinges. Mark the places for the legs – the centres are 6 cm (2¹/2 in) in from each end – and drill the holes for them. Again, do not put the legs in place yet, just make sure the holes are correct for later. You might prefer legs you can glue on or leave them off altogether.

4 Trim the Pellon on the backs of the panels to 24 cm (9¹/2 in) square and 24 cm × 49.5 cm (9¹/2 in × 19¹/2 in) respectively. Using the stapler or tacks, stretch each piece evenly over the appropriate frame piece, beginning at the centre top of one side and working to either end, then the bottom. Lastly, fasten the opposite edges, folding the corners over neatly.

5 Line the other side with the backing turning the edges under and stapling or tacking them. These staples or tacks will be covered with braid. Before putting the backing on, it would be a good idea to tack a piece of medium-weight card over the open space to give the backing fabric more support.

6 Now the hinges can be put on. Use a tapestry needle to feel the holes you made earlier, then screw on the hinges.

7 The ribbon and the nail strip can be put in place next. The nail strip also holds the ribbon in place. Fold the ends of the ribbon under so that the raw edges do not show. The nail strip will bend easily round the corners. Use its special nails to secure it. Do not put the nail strip close to the legs or you will not be able to push them in firmly.

8 Use the craft glue to secure the braid over the staples or tacks on the back. Overlap the ends of the braid. The glue will stop the braid fraying.

9 Stain or paint the knobs for the legs. Locate the holes made for the legs and carefully cut out a little circle of fabric. Push the knobs into place. Depending on the fit, you may need to use a little glue. Screw the handles on the front and attach ornamental corner pieces, if you wish.

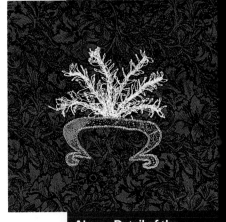

Above: Detail of the embroidery on the back.

Above: The gum blossoms are stitched in two colours.

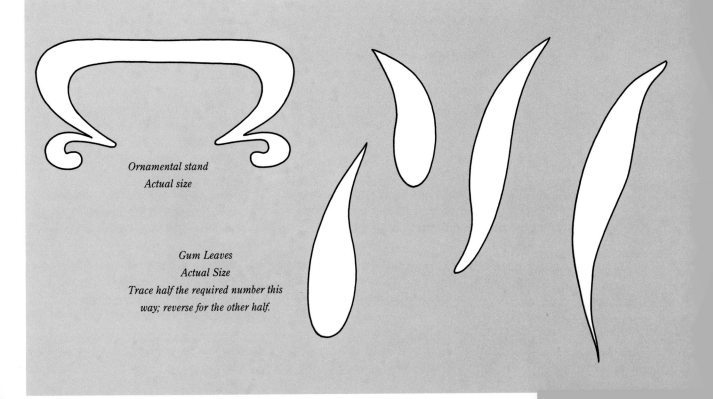

Ornamental stand
Actual size

Gum Leaves
Actual Size
Trace half the required number this way; reverse for the other half.

Laura's Quilt

'The Rabbits Flower Parade'
Just four different fabrics were used in this delicate flower and rabbit design which would delight any little person. Even the letters are decorated with tiny flowers.

The letters and rabbits are satin stitched, but all the flowers and leaves, big and small, are attached by free machine-stitching twice around them.

Finished size: 91.5 cm x 117 cm (36 in x 46 in)

CUTTING

See the pattern on page 29 and the alphabet on the Pull Out Pattern Sheet.

Begin by cutting the centre panel 60 cm x 85 cm (23¹/2 in x 33¹/2 in) lengthwise from the main fabric. Cut two strips 11.5 cm x 115 cm (4¹/2 in x 45 in) for the long borders and two strips 11.5 cm x 90 cm (4¹/2 in x 35 in) for the short borders. These measurements leave ample fabric for mitred corners on the borders.

APPLIQUE

Note: The rabbits and flowers are all taken from Block 8 (R Block) on the Medieval Inspirations Quilt. The rabbits are the same as the original size; the flowers are roughly twice the original size. The letters are half the original size.

There are approximately one hundred flowers and one hundred flower centres, and fifty-two sets of leaves along the borders, depending on the space left by the particular name.

If you wish to decorate the letters, you will need sufficient tiny flowers and leaves for one or two sets per letter.

1 Following the instructions for using Vliesofix on page 4, trace sixteen rabbits, eight facing left and eight facing right. Place the Vliesofix shapes on the back of the appliqué fabric and cut them out.

2 Arrange the rabbits, in pairs, facing away from each other in an oval shape around the central panel. The pairs parallel to the edges of the panel are approximately 5 cm (2 in) in from the edge. Place the others so that they look evenly spaced. Fuse the rabbits in position and back them with the stabiliser.

3 Satin stitch around all the rabbits.

4 Cut out and arrange thirty-two flowers and sixteen sets of leaves in a pleasing oval shape in the centre, using the Vliesofix method. The centre corners have seven flowers and three sets of leaves, with one set broken so that a single leaf trails off the design. Fuse all the flowers and leaves into place. Fuse a small circle of plain contrast fabric to the centre of each flower. Back them with the stabiliser.

5 The flowers and leaves are attached with free machine-stitching, the stem lines and extra leaves wandering between and joining the flowers together. Mark a stitching line on the quilt with a pencil or something similar. Stitch twice around each appliqué flower and leaf. The stitching is very secure and will stand up well to laundering.

6 Using a contrasting thread, possibly a metallic one, stitch the centre circles to the flowers. Tiny necklaces of flowers are appliquéd around the necks of eight rabbits and eight rabbits have bow ties. Mark in the whiskers and eyes and free machine-stitch over the marks in a colour that will stand out.

7   Cut four 4 cm (1 1/2 in) wide strips to border the centre panel and attach them, mitring the corners.

8   Cut out the letters for the name and fuse them to the borders. Satin stitch the letters on, before attaching the borders to the quilt.

9   If you want to decorate the letters, after satin stitching, cut out tiny flowers and leaves and fuse them in place, where appropriate, on the letters. Stitch them on with free machine-stitching.

Note: If the names on the top and bottom borders are the same way up, as on this quilt, then it can also be used quite successfully as a wallhanging. With a short name, you have space for a flower design on each corner. With a longer name, it might be best to put the names down the long sides only and make a flower border on the top and bottom. Think about arranging the letters so that they read down the quilt at the sides if it is hung, or just put the name on once and have a flower border the rest of the way round.

10 Attach the borders to the quilt, mitring the corners. Now the corner flowers can be fused in place and stitched. Free machine-stitch them, as for the centre ones, marking the lines lightly first, then using a contrasting colour or metallic thread to stitch the flower centres in place.

11 Cut another 4 cm (1 1/2 in) wide border and attach it to the centre panel, mitring the corners. Remove all the stabiliser from the back of the quilt top.

QUILTING

1   Assemble the three layers of the quilt following the instructions for machine-quilting on page 10.

2   Use monofilament thread through the needle and a polyester or polycotton thread to match the back of the quilt in the bobbin. Using a walking foot, quilt in the ditch around the centre panels and the borders.

3   Using a darning foot and free machine-stitching, outline the letters and rabbits, particularly accenting the legs and the ears. Next, outline the flowers, appliquéd leaves and the machine-embroidered leaves, and as you stitch, 'draw' in quilting lines, with more stems, leaves, curls and swirls loosely filling up all the blank spaces.

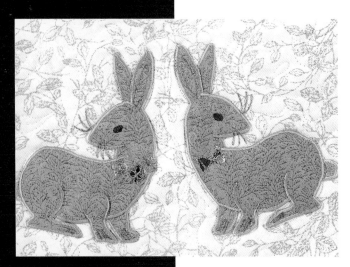

Above: Detail of the appliquéd rabbits.

Above: Detail of the border appliqué.

TO FINISH

1 Cut the binding strips 4 cm (1 1/2 in) wide and attach them to the front of the quilt, mitring the corners. Turn the binding to the back of the quilt and slipstitch it in place.

2 If you are using braid, attach it, in the ditch, around the central panel and the outside border. An open-toed embroidery foot is excellent to help guide the braid through the machine. Use a satay stick or something similar, instead of your fingers, to keep it in place. Use a zigzag stitch about 1.5 long and 1.5 mm wide and monofilament thread to stitch the braid down.

3 Make a label and add some flowers for a pretty touch on this quilt.

Above: The label awaiting the inscription.

Right: The Rabbits Flower Parade with the names arranged as for a quilt.

YOU WILL NEED

- **2 m (2¹/4 yd) of fabric for the quilt top**
- **1.5 m (1²/3 yd) of fabric for the sashing, borders and binding (cut lengthwise)**
- **1 m (1 yd) of Vliesofix**
- **1.15 m (1¹/4 yd) of iron-on stabiliser (Tearaway)**
- **20 cm (8 in) of fabric for the unicorns**
- **20 cm (8 in) of two or three fabrics for the castle**
- **10 cm (4 in) of fabric each for the leaves, flowers and creatures**
- **15 cm (6 in) of fabric for the eagle**
- **15 cm (6 in) of fabric for the name**
- **1.5 m (1²/3 yd) of fabric for the backing**
- **114 cm x 152 cm (45 in x 60 in) batting**
- **11 m (11¹/2 yd) of 6 mm (¹/4 in) wide braid (optional)**
- **rayon embroidery thread**
- **metallic thread (optional)**
- **Bobbinfil or fine polyester or polycotton thread for the bobbin**
- **monofilament thread for machine-quilting and attaching braid**
- **polyester or polycotton for the bobbin, to match the back of the quilt**
- **usual sewing supplies**
- **drawing and tracing materials**

Bryce's Quilt

'Has anybody seen my gryphons?'
This is a cot quilt made with a small boy in mind, featuring castles and exotic fanciful creatures.

Finished size: 101 cm x 127 cm (40 in x 50 in)

CUTTING

See the alphabet on the Pull Out Pattern Sheet and flowers and leaves on page 52.

Cut the central panel 62 cm x 87.5 cm (24¹/2 in x 34¹/2 in) lengthwise from the main fabric. Cut two strips 14 cm x 125 cm (5¹/2 in x 47 in) for the long borders and one long strip 14 cm x 190 cm (5¹/2 in x 75 in) to be cut in half for the short borders which will be 14 cm x 95 cm (5¹/2 in x 37¹/2 in) each.

These measurements leave ample fabric for mitred corners.

For the appliqués
Note: the patterns for this quilt are variations on the patterns used in the Medieval Inspirations Quilt.

1   Use the castle from Block 31 of the Medieval Inspirations Quilt. Enlarge the castle pattern on page 52 at 300 per cent on a photocopier. Cut out one complete castle and an extra tower each for the right- and left-hand side.

2   Trace the flowers. You will need nine for the centre panel and fifty-one for the edge design.

3   Enlarge and cut out the leaves in the same way as the flowers. You will need twelve for the centre panel and fifty-four for the edge design.

4   Use the eagle from Block 23 on the Medieval Inspirations Quilt. Enlarge the eagle pattern given on page 44 at 160 per cent on a photocopier.

5   Use the unicorns from Block 1 on the Medieval Inspirations Quilt. Enlarge the pattern given on page 22 at 200 per cent on a photocopier and cut out two unicorns, one facing each way. Cut out another two unicorns at 150 per cent, one facing each way.

6   Use the creatures from Block 11 on the Medieval Inspirations Quilt. Enlarge the pattern given on page 32 at 200 per cent on a photocopier and cut out four sets of creatures.

7   Cut out the letters for the name at the size of the pattern given.

APPLIQUE

1   Following the instructions for Vliesofix on page 4, trace the letters and the castle design. Remember to leave underlaps on one of the edges of the adjoining castle pieces. Fuse the pieces to the backs of

Above: Detail of the appliquéd unicorn.

your chosen appliqué fabrics. Depending on the number of letters in the child's name, you may have to adjust the placement of the letters, relevant to the castle design. On Bryce's Quilt, the name is centred 17 cm (6¹/₂ in) from the top edge of the centre panel. The castle is approximately 18 cm (7 in) in from either side and 20 cm (8 in) up from the bottom of the panel.

2 After fusing on the letters, back them with iron-on stabiliser and satin stitch around them. The eagle can also be stitched at this stage if you wish.

3 Fuse the castle pieces into position on the centre panel and back them with the stabiliser. Satin stitch them into place. All the other embroidery can be left until the quilt top is together.

4 Cut four strips of sashing 5 cm (2 in) wide and attach them to the centre panel, mitring the corners.

5 Trace, fuse and cut out the appliqués for the borders. Complete as much satin stitching as possible, before attaching the borders. The creatures on the top corners and the flowers and leaves on the bottom corners must be left for the next stage.

6 Attach the borders, mitring the corners.

7 Complete the rest of the appliqués, including the unicorns, flowers and leaves which cross the sashing. Complete all the satin stitching. The horns on the unicorns are also satin stitched, but their manes and tails are stitched with machine-embroidery.

EMBROIDERY

1 Complete all the embroidery either by machine or by hand, using stem stitch for the lines and French knots and lazy daisy stitch for the flower centres.

2 For the border creatures, cut small flower shapes and make a garland around each pair of creatures' necks. Attach them with free machine-stitching.

ASSEMBLING

1 Remove all the stabiliser from the back of the quilt. The outside border can now be attached. Cut it 5 cm (2 in) wide and attach it, mitring the corners.

2 Following the instructions for machine-quilting, assemble the three layers of the quilt.

QUILTING

See the gryphon quilting pattern on page 36. **Note:** This quilt was quilted by machine, but it could also be hand-quilted. For machine-quilting, use monofilament thread in

Above: The garland around the creatures' necks in the border.

Above: Detail of the gryphon quilting design.

Above: The castle is an adapted
design with extra towers added.

Above: The label for Bryce's quilt awaiting the
inscription.

the top and polyester or polycotton in the
bobbin to match the back of the quilt.

1 Begin by quilting the sashing and borders
   in the ditch, using a walking foot.
2 Using a darning foot and free machining,
   outline the castle, flowers, leaves, letters
   and unicorns.
3 Much of the quilting between the motifs
   is random or extension swirls echoing
   the embroidery. There are four gryphons
   'hidden' in the quilting. These are the
   same pattern as the gryphon on Block
   15 on the Medieval Inspirations Quilt.
   Two, one on either side of the castle
   and facing in, are 200 per cent of the
   pattern size given on page 36. Two
   smaller ones are the same size as given
   on page 36 and face each other above
   the castle. Trace the gryphons onto
   tracing paper and pin them in place on
   the quilt top. Stitch over the design and
   when the stitching is completed, tear the
   paper away.
4 The rest of the space is quilted with small
   circles placed randomly about 2.5 cm (1 in)
   apart. These also go over the gryphons
   to hide them. To do this, stitch a small
   circle with a few stitches overlapping to
   fasten it, lift the presser foot, move the
   quilt to the next spot without cutting the

threads, make another circle ... and so
on. Continue in this manner until all the
empty spaces are covered. Working
from the end, it is easy to cut the
threads which lead from one circle to
another, until all the loose threads are
snipped off. Turn to the back and repeat
the process on the back of the quilt.

TO FINISH

1 Cut the binding 4 cm (1 1/2 in) wide and
   attach it to the front of the quilt, mitring
   the corners. Turn the binding over to
   the back of the quilt and slipstitch it in
   place on the back.
2 If you are using braid, attach it in the
   ditch around the central panel and the
   outside border. An open-toed
   embroidery foot is excellent to help
   guide the braid through the machine.
   Use a satay stick or something similar,
   instead of your fingers, to keep it in
   place. Use a zigzag stitch with a stitch
   length of about 1.5 and 1.5 mm wide,
   and monofilament thread.
3 If you put a rod pocket on the back of
   the quilt, it can double as a wallhanging.

Right: Here the D Block from The
Medieval Inspirations Quilt has been
framed as a picture.

Cushion Covers

YOU WILL NEED

For one cushion

- ■ **50 cm (¹/2 yd) of fabric for the front and back**
- ■ **20 cm (8 in) square of fabric for the letter**
- ■ **at least 12.5 cm (5 in) wide pieces of different-coloured fabrics for your chosen design**
- ■ **25 cm (10 in) of Vliesofix**
- ■ **30 cm (12 in) of iron-on stabiliser (Tearaway)**
- ■ **40 cm (16 in) zipper**
- ■ **45 cm (18 in) square cushion insert**
- ■ **9 cm x 3.60 m (3¹/2 in x 4 yd) of fabric for the ruffle**
- ■ **4.5 m (5 yd) of lace or braid**
- ■ **machine-embroidery rayon threads**
- ■ **metallic threads**
- ■ **monofilament thread**
- ■ **polyester thread**
- ■ **usual sewing supplies**
- ■ **drawing and tracing materials**

Finished size: The castle and the fish cushions pictured here are 43 cm (17 in) square; the T cushion is almost 45 cm (18 in) square to accommodate the fabric design in the outer border.

Any of the blocks in the Medieval Inspirations Quilt are suitable for cushion covers. Make them up to the size you want by adding borders with or without extra appliqué. You could also enlarge the original block design and then add, or not add, borders, as required.

The castle cushion has the 26 cm (10 in) square centre from Block 25, a 1.5 cm (¹/2 in) wide border, then a 7.5 cm (3 in) wide border with twenty-eight flowers and forty leaves appliquéd in a trail around it.

The fish cushion has the 26 cm (10 in) square centre of Block 4, a 2.5 cm (1 in) wide border, then a 6.5 cm (2¹/2 in) wide border with the fish design, which has been adapted slightly to fit into it.

The T cushion has the 26 cm (10 in) square centre from Block 5, then two borders of coordinating fabrics, one 4 cm (1¹/2 in) and the other 5.5 cm (2¹/4 in) wide.

The cushion covers can be finished with lace, braid, a ruffle, piping, or a combination of these. Tassels can also be added where appropriate.

INSTRUCTIONS

See the fish appliqué pattern for the border on page 72.

Note: If you are using a central block with borders, appliqué the block first, then add the borders.

CENTRE BLOCK

1 Cut a 27 cm (10¹/2 in) square. Following the instructions for Vliesofix on page 4, trace the design and letter onto the Vliesofix. Cut them out.

2 Fuse the Vliesofix to the backs of the appliqué fabrics. Cut them out and arrange them on the block. Fuse the pieces in place.

3 Iron on the stabiliser backing.

4 Complete all the satin stitching and the machine- or hand-embroidery. For hand-embroidery, try stem or chain stitch for line work and French knots in the flowers and centres.

Above: The castle cushion features these pretty flowers in the border.

Above: The F cushion uses a brilliantly coloured fish for the centre.

5 Attach the border or borders mitring the corners. If you are using a single-edge lace or braid, it can be attached as you stitch on the borders.

6 Complete the appliqué and machine-embroidery for the borders, arranging the motifs as shown in the photograph.

7 Attach any braid trim on the centre of the cushion top, using monofilament thread through the needle and polyester thread in the bobbin, and a zigzag stitch about 1.5 long and 1.5 mm wide.

8 Remove the stabiliser from the back of the cushion top.

TO MAKE UP

1 Cut the cushion back the same width as the finished front and 1.5 cm (^{1}/$_2$ in) longer than the front.

2 Measure 10 cm (4 in) down on the long side and cut the fabric into two pieces at that point (the cut runs between the long sides). This is the zipper opening.

3 Pin and stitch the back pieces together, approximately 2.5 cm (1 in) from each end, to form an enclosed opening for the zipper. Stitch in the zipper.

4 Make sure the front and back are the same size, then round off the corners to make it easier to attach the ruffle or single-edge braid. Fold the 9 cm (3^1/$_2$ in) wide ruffle strip exactly in half lengthwise and press. Using a gathering thread or the ruffle attachment on the machine, gather the fabric up to half its length. Baste the ruffle to the right side of the cushion front, easing it around the corners. Turn the raw edges of the ruffle on each end to the inside and overlap them a little.

5 Leaving the zipper partly open, place the back of the cushion and the top together with the right sides facing and the ruffle sandwiched in between. Stitch around the edge, making sure that the ruffle is lying flat towards the centre of the cushion cover.

6 Turn the cushion cover through the zipper opening and round out the corners. Press.

7 Attach braid around the inside edge of the ruffle.

8 Slip the cushion insert inside and close the cover.

The Z Flower Quilt

This design is taken from Block 2 (Z Block) on the Medieval Inspirations Quilt. It is almost the same as the full block on the quilt, except that the centre has been changed a little so that the design fits neatly into a 25.5 cm (10 in) square.

Finished size: 117 cm × 142 cm (46 in × 56 in)
Block size: 25.5 cm (10 in)
Number of blocks: 12

CUTTING

See the block design and the quilting patterns on the Pull Out Pattern Sheet.

1 Cut two lengthwise strips 13 cm × 140 cm (5¹/2 in × 55 in) for the long borders and two lengthwise strips 13 cm × 114 cm (5¹/2 in × 45 in) for the short borders. These measurements leave ample fabric for mitred corners.

2 From the piece of fabric left, cut twelve 28 cm (11 in) squares. Appliqué tends to distort the blocks, so they will be cut back to 26.5 cm (10¹/2 in) later.

APPLIQUE

Note: Each block has twelve flowers. There are four different leaves in each block – sixteen in total. The centre four are all the same. For the corner sets of three leaves, you will need two facing one way and two facing the other.

For the border, each cluster of flowers has six flowers and one set of six leaves, with half facing each way. The border has forty-eight flowers and eight sets of leaves.

1 Following the method for using Vliesofix on page 4, trace the flowers and leaves required. Fuse the Vliesofix onto the

back of the appliqué fabrics. Cut out the flower appliqués from the length of the fabric, leaving the other long side intact for the sashing and borders.

2 Arrange the flower and leaf appliqués on the blocks and fuse them in place. Back the blocks with iron-on stabiliser.

3 Complete all the satin stitching.

4 Mark in the lines for the free machine-embroidery very lightly with a pencil, dressmaker's pencil or similar, then stitch over them. Alternatively, hand-embroider them with stem stitch.

5 Complete all twelve blocks, then remove all the stabiliser from the back of the blocks, being careful not to pull the embroidery as you do so.

ASSEMBLING

1 Square up the blocks and cut them to exactly 26.5 cm (10¹/2 in) square.

2 Cut the sashing 4 cm (1¹/2 in) wide and join all the blocks together with sashing in between, being careful to place them all the same way, as the two sets of opposite sides are different. Put one last row of sashing right round the blocks.

For the borders

1 Trace and cut out the flowers and leaves for the borders. Fuse in place the ones in the centre of each border. Back the border behind the appliqués with the stabiliser, then complete the stitching and embroidery.

2 Attach the borders to the blocks, mitring the corners. The corner flowers can now be fused into position, backed with stabiliser and stitched.

3 When all the stitching and embroidery

YOU WILL NEED
Note: The materials given are for the quilt as photographed, but it can be made as big or as small as required, with or without sashing.

- ■ 2.5 m (2²/3 yd) of fabric for the blocks and borders
- ■ 1.5 m (1²/3 yd) of fabric for the sashings, borders, binding and appliqués
- ■ 20 cm (8 in) of fabric for the flower centres
- ■ 40 cm (16 in) of green fabric for the leaves
- ■ 2.4 m (2¹/3 yd) of fabric for the backing (this will have to be cut and joined)
- ■ 1 m (1 yd) of Vliesofix
- ■ 1.25 m (1¹/2 yd) of iron-on stabiliser (Tearaway)
- ■ 130 cm × 150 cm (50 in x 60 in) of batting
- ■ 18 m (19¹/2 yd) of 6 mm (¹/4 in) wide braid for the sashings and outer border
- ■ 5.3 m (5³/4 yd) of 2 cm (³/4 in) wide braid for the outer edge
- ■ monofilament thread
- ■ polyester thread
- ■ usual sewing supplies
- ■ drawing and tracing materials

have been completed, remove the stabiliser from the back of the quilt top.

4 Cut the sashing 4 cm (1½ in) wide and attach it to the border.

QUILTING

1 Following the instructions for machine-quilting on page 10, pin the three layers of the quilt together.

2 Using a walking foot, monofilament thread through the needle and a polyester or polycotton thread to match the back of the quilt in the bobbin, complete all the straight-line quilting. Begin at the centre top and work out to the edge one way, then turn the quilt and, again beginning at the centre, work out to the opposite edge. Turn the quilt 90 degrees and work the third quarter; then after another 90 degree turn, all the straight-line stitching will be completed.

3 Lower the feed dogs and, using the darning foot, outline the flowers and leaves. Work one whole block at a time and stitch in some extra quilted leaves or lines to fill any spaces.

4 The sprays of flowers and leaves on the borders are quilted in the same manner. For the large border spaces, trace the quilting designs onto tracing paper. Pin

the paper in place on the border and stitch over it. When all the stitching is completed, tear the paper away.

TO FINISH

1 Cut the binding 4 cm (1½ in) wide and attach it to the right side of the quilt top, mitring the corners. Turn the binding to the back of the quilt and slipstitch it in place.

2 If you are using braid, attach it in the ditch around all the edges of the sashing. An open-toed embroidery foot is excellent to help guide the braid through the machine. Use a satay stick or something similar, instead of your fingers, to keep it in place. Stitch the braid on one way right across the central strips, then across the first braid at right angles. Begin and end the strips where they will be covered by the braid on the edge of the sashing. This can be put on in a continuous piece, so there is only one join. Braid is also stitched on both sides of the appliquéd border. The wide braid on the edge is stitched on over the completed binding. Use monofilament thread to zigzag the braid in place with a machine setting of length 1.5 and 1.5 mm wide.

Above: Detail of a block.

Above: Detail of the quilting in the borders.

Bolster

The bolster design is taken directly from Block 7 on the Medieval Inspirations Quilt. Repeating the design three times fits perfectly around the bolster.

INSTRUCTIONS
For the panels
Note: Each panel is 18 cm (7 in) wide and 35.5 cm (14 in) long. Use the lengthwise grain of the fabric around the bolster for a firm fit. That means the three design panels have their length on the crosswise grain of the fabric.

1   Find the centre of the fabric and, keeping the grain line in mind, mark out the three panels. You should have a seam allowance left on the two long sides of the design and approximately 7.5 cm (3 in) on either end for gathering the ends of the bolster.

2   Following the instructions for using Vliesofix on page 4, trace three sets of the design. Fuse the Vliesofix pieces to the backs of the appliqué fabrics. Cut them out and arrange them on the bolster fabric.

3   Fuse the design in place. Fuse the Tearaway stabiliser onto the back of your work. It may be easier to stabilise, then stitch, one block at a time.

YOU WILL NEED
- 51 cm x 55 cm (20 in x 21¹/2 in) of fabric
- 10 cm (4 in) of two different fabrics for the appliqués
- small scraps of another fabric for the centre flowers
- 45 cm (18 in) cushion insert
- 60 cm (24 in) of calico
- 2.3 m (2¹/2 yd) of braid and/or ribbon (I used 6 mm (¹/4 in) wide braid and 2 cm (³/4 in) wide ribbon)
- rayon embroidery threads
- metallic threads
- monofilament thread
- two tassels or 1.25 m (1¹/4 yd) of cord
- 40 cm (16 in) of Vliesofix
- 50 cm (20 in) of iron-on stabiliser (Tearaway)
- small piece of iron-on Vilene (for Finishing Method 2)
- usual sewing supplies
- drawing and tracing materials

4 Complete all the satin stitching and machine-embroidery. If you are embroidering by hand, stem stitch would look good with French knots in the centre of the flowers.

5 Remove all the stabiliser from the back of the panels. Attach the braid and or ribbon around the panel edges. The bolster shown has a 2 cm ($3/4$ in) wide ribbon with 6 mm ($1/4$ in) braid on top of it. They were stitched on together with a zigzag stitch of about 1.5 length and 1.5 mm width, using monofilament thread in the top and polyester thread in the bobbin. Stitch the lines dividing the designs first, positioning the line near the seam so that when the seam is stitched closed, the seam will be hidden under or right beside the braid. Stitch the ribbon and braid on the length of the bolster, covering the raw ends of the first three strips of braid and ribbon.

6 With right sides together, join the seam across the width of the bolster.

For the bolster insert

This is made by folding the purchased cushion insert in half and making a casing for it out of the calico.

1 Cut a piece of calico 35.5 cm × 55 cm (14 in × 21$1/2$ in). Fold the calico with the right sides together and machine-stitch the 35.5 cm (14 in) side, leaving a gap in the centre large enough to insert the cushion insert.

2 Cut two 15.5 cm (6 in) diameter circles of calico and stitch one circle into either end of the bolster casing, easing the two pieces to fit together. Turn the casing right side out.

3 Fold the cushion insert in half and slip it into the casing. Slipstitch the opening closed.

TO FINISH

Note: There are two ways to finish the bolster; either way, you may have to trim a little off each end of the bolster cover for a snug fit.

Method 1: Stitch a casing on each end and thread a cord through it. Pull up the cord to gather in the end and tie it in a bow. This way you will be able to take the cover off to launder it.

Method 2: Cut two 6.5 cm (2$1/2$ in) diameter circles of fabric and two 5 cm (2 in) diameter circles of iron-on Vilene. Centre the two Vilene circles inside the fabric circles. Using a running stitch, gather up the 6 mm ($1/4$ in) seam allowance and secure. Attach a tassel to the centre of each circle. Hand-stitch the circles with the tassels over the gathered ends to finish the bolster.

Bibliography

Henry Shaw, *Alphabets and Numbers of the Middle Ages*, Studio Editions Ltd, 1994

Christopher de Hamel, *A History of Illuminated Manuscripts*, Phaidon Press Ltd, 1994

A Medieval Christmas, Harper Collins Publishers in association with the British Library, 1996

John Harthan, *Books of Hours*, Thames and Hudson, 1978

D. M. Gill, *Illuminated Manuscripts*, Brockhampton Press, 1996

Margaret Manion and Vera Vines, *Medieval and Renaissance Illuminated Manuscripts*, Thames and Hudson, 1984

Barty Phillips, *Tapestry*, Phaidon Press Ltd, 1994

Bernard Meehan, *Book of Kells*, Thames and Hudson, 1994

Timothy Noad and Patricia Seligman, *The Illuminated Alphabet*, Simon and Schuster, 1994

Donald King and Santina Levey, *The Victoria and Albert Museum's Textile Collection*, Embroidery in Britain from 1200 to 1750, Canopy Books, 1993

W. & G. Audsley, *Victorian Sourcebook of Medieval Decoration*, Dover Publications, 1991